Library of Congress-in-Publication Data:
Monique R. Ransom
ISBN-978-0615780092

Who Is Thy Neighbor?

A Real Look at the Heart of the
Christian Soul!

Monique R. Ransom

If any man say, I Love God, and his brother, he is a
liar; for he that loveth not his brother whom he hath
seen, how can he love God whom he hath not seen?

An this commandment have we from him, That he
who loveth God love his brother also
1 John 4:20-21

TABLE OF CONTENT

Acknowledgements

There are many people who have made sacrifices for the sake of this book. Many of whom I cannot mention in order to protect their identity: to all of you I say thank-you. Without you, this story could not be told.

There are others who have also made a significant impact on my life as well as on the completion of this book, and I would like to take the opportunity to acknowledge them now:

To my children, Renee, the late Trenton Jr., Tyrone, and Sierra, who again watched Mommy work endless days and tiresome nights to accomplish the vision God has given to her: All of you have been the driving force in my life. I love you!

To my closest and dearest friend who stands by my side at the times I needed her the most and even when I didn't. My true Samaritans in Christ, Sherian K. Anderson.

Hey Daddy! Your little girl is growing-up! This is a special Thank-you to my dad, Bruce C. Ransom Jr., for the support and encouragement throughout time: I love ya!

To all who have supported me over the years: I thank-you and ask that you continue to keep my family in your prayers always.

To all the Levites, Priests, and Good Samaritans of the world: to God be all the glory.

Introduction

In The Beginning

Destination…………………Eternal Life

Mission……………………To Save The World

Called……………………To Be A Light In Darkness

Sometimes we get blinded from the true meaning of why we have been redeemed. Caught up in an old mind set of traditions, set by men, we become unseeing of the truth that is right in front of us. Yes, God did send His Son, Jesus, as a ransom for us, but He also planned that, we, through our redemption, would help one another get to the final destination called Eternal Life (**John 3:16-17**). It is while we are on this journey to our eternal destination that we are given one mission, and that is to save the world. We do this by becoming lights in the midst of a dark world (**John 1:4, 5**) and (**Matthew 5:14**).

How do we become this light and what does being a light mean? We become the lights by obeying the commandments that Jesus left for us to follow.

From them, we learn and help each other to learn also.

There is an old adage that says- "Each One, Teach One." This is an excellent statement that demonstrates how we can learn from one another (Matthew 7:12). Unfortunately, learning is taking place, but much of what is learned are heresies. Heresies are beliefs or opinions contrary to doctrine. Now I use that term doctrine loosely because man has also created many doctrines and because of this we have internalized many false beliefs, have performed many false practices, and this produces contaminated thinking.

Many of those redeemed of the Lord have become like the world. You cannot tell us apart at times. We have become so cold and hard-hearted towards each other that when the world sees us, they see an image of what they are trying to be delivered from. If each Christian took a little more concern for the other as we have been commanded to do, we would not have so much gossiping and backbiting with all sorts of wickedness in churches and in hearts today.

The key to it all is Love! It is through love that we become the true lights of God. Love is the only thing that can separate us from the world. It is the only way to recognize God's people. God tells us that we will know his people by their love (**John 13:34-35**).

Maybe, just maybe, if we remember this when the time comes for us to help each other, God will be able to draw more men unto himself; but instead, people look at our fruit and see that we are no different than they are. This should not be.

Although this is not true for all of us, for most of us it is. Many of us need to examine our lives closer to determine how much of God's nature, which is love, we truly possess. We will be amazed how far we are from reaching the place God wants us to be.

1 Corinthians 13: 4-8 tells us that *love* is kind, gentle, does not envy, is not puffed up, does not behave rudely, does not seek its own, not provoked to think evil, does not rejoice in iniquity, but rejoices in the truth; does not parade itself.

Love never fails, it bears all things, believes all things, hopes all things, endures all things, but there are other components to love that are also mentioned throughout the Bible that teach us that love is also patient, compassionate, sympathetic, longsuffering, and sacrificial. It is that simple! The Word of God has called us to serve one another through love (**Galatians 5:13**).

Who Is Thy Neighbor? takes a real hard look at the heart of the Christian soul. It is from the heart, **Proverbs 4:23** tells us that all the issues of life flows. In this book, we will examine some of those issues. Issues that have kept many of us from reaching that place God has called us to be.

The Bible tells us to examine ourselves daily **(2 Cor. 13:5**) so that we may catch those things that try to attach themselves to us as we journey through this natural life. The Word of God is like a surgeon —It cleans, purges, and cuts all manner of wickedness and evil spirits that seek to destroy us. That is why we must stay in the Work of God; reading, praying, and fasting so that we may be able to stand against the wiles of our enemies.

Our adversary is well versed in the knowledge of God. It is us who must learn so that he has no place in our lives. The Bible says that God's people suffer for lack of knowledge. Knowledge of who God is and what He wants us to do must become our focus and our drive (**2 Timothy 3:15-17**). That same drive most of us use to be successful in this life.

This book conveys a real life story using a fictional character named Jasmine. Jasmine is a representation of all our lives at one time or another as well as someone's life we might know. In this story, Jasmine's life depicts the parable that Jesus told the disciples concerning the Good Samaritan
(**Luke 10:25-37**).

Many of us have read, preached, and even taught this parable, but yet its meaning still eludes many of us as to what God truly requires from us when He commands us to love one another. If we are to be the lights God has called us to be, here is a good place to start. We will discover some good things about ourselves as well as some areas that need improvement.

For how can we love God, if we hate our brother (**1 John 4:20**). Is this not what the Word of God tells us? God wants us to rise above our petty selfishness and get to the place where He can give us more, knowing that what He gives us will not control us. Freely are the gifts God has given us and freely does He want us to offer them to others: the prospect of everlasting life (**John 17:3**), divine protection (**Psalm 145:18-20**), and free access to God in prayer (**Psalm 65:2**).

We are not limited to just spiritual gifts, but everything we are, own, love, and cherish are gifts as well. One of our most challenging gifts are "Material Things and Money!" This is an area that the enemy constantly defeats most of us because of the lust of our flesh and our desires for riches more than God. It will also be our destruction, if we don't wake up and become wise about what God want us to know about these things.

Let us begin to examine what these things might be as we read about the life of a woman named Jasmine.

Lord,
I pray that all those who read this book will receive
from you the heart of Christ.
The Author

Chapter 1

UNDERSTANDING YOUR SEASON OF CHANGE!

"To everything there is a season, a time for every purpose under heaven: A time to be born and a time to die; A time to plant and a time to pluck what is planted; A time to kill and a time to heal; A time to break down and a time to build up; A time to weep and a time to laugh; A time to mourn and a time to dance; a time to cast away stones and a time to gather stones; A time to embrace and a time to refrain from embracing; A time to gain and a time to lose; A time to keep and a time to throw away; A time to tear and a time to sew; A time to keep silence and a time to speak; a time to love and a time to hate; A time of war and a time of peace." Ecclesiastes 3:1

No matter what season you are in currently, remember that God is willing and are able to bring you through. You must come to realization and forever settle in your heart that God has created everything beautiful in its time.

In this chapter, you will learn about seasons and the things that take place during those seasons. Notice that the scripture talks about how God has a time for every purpose under the heaven (Ecclesiastes **3:1-8**). This lets you know right away that life will have many thrills and frills, lows and highs. God is simply preparing you for these necessary changes that you must make. He is letting you know not to get too comfortable in life being just one way. God, however, did promise you a safe journey, but not a calm passage (**Deut. 4:30**).

We all hope for laughter, joy, and peace every day of our lives, but scripture tells us that life in this present system of things will not always be this way. If we live long enough, life will show us that same thing. Why? Because God has deemed life to have tribulations (**John 16:33**). There will be good times and bad times too! Times when we will have plenty and times when we will lack. The only thing that stays constant in our lives, or at least should, is God.

He the same yesterday, today, and forevermore (**Hebrews 13:8**). He changes not. We change! Some of us for the good and some of us for the bad; but, whatever change we make, we are changing nevertheless.

CHANGE! That is what disturbs us the most. Change is necessary if we want to grow spiritually to the place God has called us to be. You would think by now that many of us would be quite use to *change*. It is in this year of our Lord and Savior Jesus Christ, that change will become the main ingredient to our very survival. The true Christians will have to make the necessary *changes* in their lives in order to receive from God the promises that He has made to them (**Galatians 3:10-29**).

We have now entered a time period where we must be willing to *change* or die. I am not talking about death to just the natural body; although, for some that will be the case, but I am talking about death to the spirit- The same death Adam and Eve faced in the Garden of Eden when they pulled mankind into sin because of disobedience.

Time is drawing nigh and the return of Christ is soon to come. He needs true Christians to be at their fullest potential, in Him, in order for them to accomplish the great commission (**Matthew 28:19-20**). He is preparing His armies to march forward. It is the time of the true Christians. All things now point in the direction of His great return, and we, the children of God, must step up to the plate. We must be willing to let go of petty issues over spiritual matters (which by the way God told us not to argue over in the first place (**2 Timothy 2:14**) that divide us and keep us separate (**Mark 3:25**). We must set aside all those weights that have us bound and release all our cares upon Him (**1 Peter 5:7**). We must be willing and able to examine those darken areas of our lives that have gone unforgotten by us and hath yielded forth no fruit. It is time to mature; to let go of the milk. We can no longer afford to remain milk drinkers of His word, saved by grace but still reflecting every bit of the world's nature (**1 Peter 2:2**).

It is not our acceptance of Christ that makes our enemies nervous, it is the knowledge of God's truth (**1Timothy 2:4**). Satan knows that once we give ourselves completely to God and allow His truth to reign through every crevice of our mortal bodies, we will become unstoppable. He will no longer be able to fool us with those smoke screens that are often thrown away. He knows that we will arise with power and authority.

Our enemies are gearing up for the battle, and we must too. They will do anything and everything to stop true Christians from moving in the direction of God's command. If we are mature Christians then we know that our enemy is already defeated. Many of us don't; therefore growth will be necessary. Otherwise, we will be tossed around with the wind by every trick and deception that our adversary throws our way (**Ephesians 4:14**). We must prepare for quick maturity and become bold. No longer will God wait for us to mature over the same issues that He has been trying to get us to *change*. He has spent enough time striving with us over these things (**Genesis 6:3**). When you hear His voice, *move*. When you feel his convictions, *change*. It is that simple.

Our enemies will look to detain us by stopping our

growth by putting us through many temptations to lure us away from God. Obstacles will he place in front of us to trip us up and keep us stumbling all the days of our lives. Our adversary knows that *change* is important to our spiritual growth. That through change we will be able to move to higher levels and deeper dimensions in Christ where those once hidden truths no longer remain hidden to us (**Proverbs 2:4-7**).

God desires to take us behind the veil and into the "Holies of Holies" (**Hebrews 10:19-20**), but not without the necessary changes in our lives. God doesn't just let anyone come behind the veil (**Hebrews 6:19**), but let some tell you they go behind everyday. This is still a sacred place not open to just anyone and everyone just because they confess Jesus Christ. Our confession gives us access that was once denied thought sin but now open through salvation, so what sins closed salvation reopened.

In the Old Testament only the high priest could come there (**Exodus 19:22**). Today, our High Priest is Jesus Christ, but because of Christ we are now able to come.

Jesus' sacrifice opened the way of approach to God (**Ephesians 3:11-12**). We must present our bodies a living sacrifice, holy and acceptable unto God (**Romans 12:1**), and in order to complete these things, we must change.

Our lives will never remain constant because life is filled with seasons that go up and down. However, we should enter each season with joy, no matter the kind, knowing that God's promise of victory for us is always true. The Word tells us that we will reap in due season if we faint not (Galatians 6:5). This means that we must hold on to Truth and endure if we want to receive the harvest from our labor.

Psalm 55:19 tells us about the necessity of change and how God feels about it

God will hear, and afflict them, Even He who abides from of old. Se'lah.
Because they do not change, Therefore they do not fear God.

Psalm 55:19

What does this mean? It means those of us who do not *change* have no fear or reverence of God in our lives. God says that it is our fear of Him that shows the beginning of knowledge (**Proverbs 1:7**).

Only fools despise wisdom and instruction, but because of their lack of fear for God, He promises to afflict them, and he doesn't care how old you are (**Psalm 37:9**). Solomon was one of the wisest kings that this earth will ever come to know because he sought wisdom, God gave him riches beyond measure. A lesson that we can all learn: God says in **Proverbs 1:5**, "A wise man will hear and increase his learning and a man of understanding will attain wise counsel."

As Christians, *change* should be nothing new to us because we are changed when we accept Christ as our Lord and Savior. This *change*, as you should know, is not an outward change, but an inward change. Our hearts of stone are *changed* to hearts of flesh (Ezekiel 36:26). Moldable and pliable for the potter to work with.

Some of us remain pliable by the renewing of our minds while others become harden once again (**2 Corinthians 5:17-21**) because we won't allow the renewing to have its perfect work in us.

Change is often brought through trials and tribulations. We take on more of the characteristics of Christ as we go through them. It is also through them we are perfected. *Change* is alarming for most. This is why so many of us still resist change. If we decide to *change*, we have to deal with unfamiliar territory; Virgin ground that has not been touched by us, can be upsetting to most. Most times, we don't know what will happen to us, so we would rather stay where we are than go through the necessary changes.

In order for us to relate to the necessary changes that must take place in our lives, we will examine the life of a woman named Jasmine. Jasmine a woman called by God enters a season where she is faced with much difficulty. Will she submit to the *changes* that God is leading her to make or will she resist them? Let us take a look at the story.

The Story Begins

Long ago while facing a difficult moment in her life, the Lord God presented Jasmine with this question:

"Who is thy neighbor?"

It puzzled Jasmine as to why God would ask her this question, especially during such a difficult moment in her life. Not truly knowing where to apply this question, Jasmine figured that it must have something to do with what was currently going on in her life at that moment. First, she began to examine her life in relationship to the question proposed by God.

She replied,

"Lord which neighbor are you talking about? The one on the left or the one on the right?"

He replied with,

"Both of them and many more like them."

Afterwards, God led her to reread the story about the Good Samaritan.

Now, Jasmine knew the story about the Good Samaritan. She had read it many times before.
She figured that there must have been something hidden in this parable of scripture that she missed and now God is trying to show her what it is. As God was, once again, passing on some of His magnificent wisdom, Jasmine tried to recall the story from memory and could not understand what God wanted her to know. Finally, she did as God requested and went back to reread the story.

Lesson Break:
Jasmine should have been obedient and did what God told her to do from the beginning, but like most of us, she tried to do it her way. It is this process that messes things up for us all the time. We often make matters worse and then what happens? We end up going right back and doing it the way God told us to do it in the first place. Jasmine thought that her memory of the story would do, but this is not what God told her to do.
If God wanted her to recall the story from memory,

He would have said that, but He did not. He instructed Jasmine to reread it instead and that is what she ended up doing.

What is the lesson?

Do what God tells you to do the first time.

Well, Jasmine began to reread the story about the Good Samaritan. She read it over and over again, until she realized what God wanted to show her was right in her own trial.

This story of the Good Samaritan was a replica of Jasmine's present day circumstances and situations. As you go through your trials and tribulations you will often find that there are circumstances in the Bible that others have incurred that is similar to your situations. You will realize that circumstances that others have gone through may apply to your everyday life; some situations that parallel our very own lives. This was one of hers; the story of the Good Samaritan.

Who were these neighbors that surrounded Jasmine at this point in her life? Well, they weren't just the neighbors who lived on the left and right of her. They were all of the people that God chose to surround Jasmine both day and night. They were ones she knew, ones who knew her, and ones that she did not know.

They were friends-saved and unsaved, family members, pastors, deacons, mothers of the church onlookers. They represented the congregations, the choirs, and the usher boards. They were anyone and everyone who has passed through Jasmine's path of life in some form or fashion. Maybe you overheard her situations through a friend, a co-worker or a neighbor. Maybe you saw her at church, on the bus or in the neighborhood. Maybe you visited her every day or just one day; either way you were considered Jasmine's neighbor. It doesn't matter how you met her or if you didn't you were her neighbor because God made you aware of her somehow.

The characters in this story are real people whose names have been changed to protect the innocent and the guilty. This story is to all of you who can recall a similar situation in your life or in the life of someone else. This story is to those who are currently neighboring someone else and are not aware of it. This story is for the churches in Christ whose job is to be the Good Samaritan and the good neighbor. I dedicate this story to you.

The fear of the Lord is the beginning
of knowledge, But fools despise
wisdom and discipline.
Proverbs 1:7

The Good Samaritan

A certain man went down from Jerusalem to Jericho, and fell among thieves, which stripped him of his raiment, and wounded him, departed leaving him half dead.

And by chance there came down a certain priest that way: and when he saw him, he passed by on the other side.

And likewise a Levite, when he was at the place, came and looked on him, and passed by on the other side.

But a certain Samaritan, as he journeyed, came where he was and when he saw him, he had compassion on him,

And went to him, and bound up his wounds, pouring oil and wine, and set him on his own beast, and brought him to an inn, and took care of him.

And on the morrow when he departed, he took out two pence, and gave them to the innkeeper, and said unto him. Take care of him; and whatsoever thou spendest more, when I come again, I will repay thee.

Which now of these three, thinkest thou, was neighbor unto him that fell among thieves?

And he said, "He that shewed mercy on him." Then Jesus unto him, "go and do thou likewise."

Luke 10:25-37

Chapter 2

THE CHALLENGE

Approximately 12 years ago, Jasmine was facing one of the most life-changing and challenging circumstances in her life, and that was putting it mildly. From those years, seven of them were spent in trial that God used to train, teach, and provide wisdom to Jasmine about who He really is and how much He loves His people.

Now, you do know that God will allow this. If you don't you know it now. Although God tempts no man, He will test them. God will allow Satan to test us just so that He can prove us worthy. Look at the life of Job and Abraham which only names a few. Each of them was placed in hard places. Places that many of us hope to never walk. In the case of Job, which we should all be familiar with, it was God who asked Satan what he was doing and if he has considered His servant Job. God initiated the test that Job was not prepared for and Satan did not plan (**Job 1:1-12**) but wanted to for many years. This was Satan's golden opportunity to touch one of

God's anointed.

Jasmine is now in the same place as Job. God has placed her in the wilderness to be tested, as Jesus was for forty days in the wilderness. She is about to face her enemies. Enemies she has never known before this day. This is her test of destiny.

It is from one segment of her seven year trial that Jasmine, led by the Spirit of the Lord, reveals to us that greater knowledge can be brought to the true Christians about being a Good Samaritan and good neighbor one to another.

Those seven years that Jasmine refers to were hard and difficult times. Her marriage was falling apart; money was relatively nonexistent, and self-esteem was mighty low. She had to do one of the most difficult things known to man, and that was trust in God. A God she barely knew, and a God she could not see. A God, up until a year ago, was just a spirit in heaven; someone that you prayed to when things got bad and forgot about when things were good. She did not know God.

All she knew was that she walked down as isle and surrendered her life a little more than 12 months ago. It was her time to know Him for the God He was, is, and will forever be.

Lesson Break:
Yes, you read it correctly, Jasmine had a difficult time trusting in God and we all do. Let me be real with, you, right now! Trusting in God is not easy to do especially as a new Christian unfamiliar with God's ways, unskillful in spiritual warfare, and just downright unknowledgeable in the Word. Plus, it is hard enough to trust man, needless to say, God.

Why?

Well, we tend to treat God the same way we deal with people to begin with, how do you suppose we will able to just trust God? This trust factor is a process that comes over a time and through *change*. Why do we pretend so much that trusting is easy? I do not know. Maybe we want others to think that we got it all together when we don't. All I can say is that it is difficult, but with time trusting God gets a lot easier to do.

So I know how Jasmine felt. Coming from a past that had developed many trust issues made it even harder for me to trust in a God I did not see and barely knew. Getting saved does not automatically cure you from all the issues you had before you accepted Christ. We transfer all our issues over to God and God through love, mercy, and grace will transform us, if we let Him.

As for Jasmine, she was just beginning to know God. She always knew that He existed, but she never had a relationship with Him. She got saved about one year prior to these circumstances in her life. Jasmine had moved around so much as a military wife that she wasn't really rooted and grounded in God's Word which is necessary for mature growth in God. In addition, Jasmine wasn't constantly In the fellowship of other believers. Consequently, she was trying to communicate with God based upon the old mind sets and inadequate denominational training, Jasmine was in no way prepared for what she was now facing.

Jasmine had to learn firsthand. Most of her wisdom and knowledge came from reading the Word of God; the Bible, but the *Rhema* came from an intimate relationship with God. God also provided knowledge for her through cassette taped ministry sermons, television sermons, and then right when the trial really began to rear its ugly head, God blessed her to have someone in her life, as a friend, who would teach her more about whom God was and how He cared for her.

God began to equip her for the journey. These tools that would guide her and teach her many great things. They would assist in opening up her eyes to God's true Kingdom of righteousness and all the wonderful things that come with it.

The Lesson

During this period, God wanted Jasmine to learn how to trust Him and I mean *really trust Him*. God allowed all of her doors of opportunities to be shut for a season.

It was also during that season that her marriage was beginning to fall apart. As a result, Jasmine felt upset and confused about why this was beginning to happen to her.

And to the angel of the church in Philadelphia write; these things saith he hath that is holy, he that is true, he that hath the key of David, he that openeth, and no man shutteth; and shutteth, and no man openeth;….
Revelation 3:8

Unfortunately, this was not the very beginning of her trial. This trial began in California when Jasmine slowly began to learn the tools for spiritual warfare and where God imparted His Holy Spirit filled with wisdom to help her to endure. The one girlfriend that God placed in her life, Lisa, in California, imparted more than just God's wisdom and gift. Into Jasmine, she also imparted her prophetic mantle in which Jasmine was totally unaware of.

How did this come to be? This will be revealed a little later on in the book

Let's Continue...

When Jasmine and her family had left California she thought that the trial was over, but soon realized that she was now entering a new phase of the trial, just in a new place. Jasmine blamed God for her marriage going wrong. She did not know that God was using this situation in her life to strengthen her.

Many of us do not know that God will use any natural situations we encounter, those that are common to man, to build us up spiritually?

Going back to Job, God once said that we have focused many sermons on what Job lost and what he gains but not on what God allowed to be touched.

In other words, there is nothing in our lives that's not expendable to God for use in our spiritual growth. When I say NOTHING! I mean NOTHING! Many Christian's don't believe that. They have this picture of God as this simple minded man who is senile, and does only what we call good deeds.

Well here is a rude awaking, things that we sometimes consider bad is sometimes good to God. I know we don't want to hear that but it is true none the less. Look at Job's life. The only area he instructed Satan not to touch is death. He could not take Job's life but he could touch his relationship with his wife and friends. He could touch his finances and livelihood. He could touch the lives of his children and cattle. He finally allowed Satan to touch his health as well.

I know, I know, that seems almost contradictory to healing beliefs, but again it is true nonetheless. God will allow the enemy access to areas He has already designed in our plan for mature growth. It is as simple as that although uncomfortable in thought. He tempts o man but He darn sure does TEST them and a whole lot of them too!

There hath no temptation taken you but such as is common to man: but God is faithful, who will not suffer you to be tempted above that ye are able; but will with the temptation also make a way of escape, that ye may be able to bear it
1 Corinthians 10:13

This trial, however created by man's own lust, became the center point in which God would create a spiritually, mature woman. It was Jasmine's double-minded lustful husband that brought instability into their home and yet an opportunity for God (**James 1:8**). It is man's own lust for the things of this world that lures him into the tempter's den of temptations (**James 1:14**). However, it was Jasmine's love for her husband that led her trust in God for restoration of her family.

It was this trial that God used to begin stripping and crucifying much of Jasmine's flesh. Who knows if she will emerge to be a strong and virtuous woman of God? God knows; that's who. Jasmine was the clay in God's mighty hands. Let's begin Jasmine's journey with God, not knowing how this would unfold in her life.

The Setup!

Now, let's take a look at Jasmine's situation. She was facing a failing marriage with three children and one on the way. A marriage that grew cold and harsh.

On top of it, she was in a new city where she received very little help from those she expected could help her. At first, God made sure that she had very little to no one to turn to, but Him. He shut the door which would lead her to having a job to support herself and her family. He had hardened the hearts of the only two relatives that lived there who were destined not to be too much of a help for her anyhow. She was coming close to having nothing and I mean nothing. The little bit of money that she saved, was going fast. She could not find a job anywhere and it was not for the lack of trying.

Reality Check Time!

I don't know about you, but she was carrying quite a bit on her plate. If you think that the whole world was on her shoulders, you are right because it was; at least that's how it felt to Jasmine. That world she carried was that of her family because she had no one naturally to turn to and that is the way God had planned it to be.

Her walls were closing in around her and she felt surrounded by the pressures of life. She felt unable to breathe in this situation.

She just knew she would pass out and faint at any given moment.

Then, one day out of mad frustration, Jasmine said, "Lord, what is going on here? You know I can't find work anywhere. Please help me find a job." Every application from everywhere got lost or misplaced. It was a mess! She had applied for work as a teacher which was her practicing profession, but could not get hired. Jasmine had worked as a teacher in, her home state New Jersey for 5 years before she came to Maryland. Maryland was desperately looking for teachers so her chances should have greatly increased, but they didn't. For some reason they could never seem to find the paperwork that she had submitted. Even when she had hand delivered it herself, it still got misplaced. Everything that Jasmine sent out, mailed or hand delivered was either lost or misplaced. Nothing seemed to go right.

How many of you can identify with her? Think about the times in your life when everything seemed to go wrong. I know I can think of many myself. So many that I felt like screaming. So,

Jasmine cried out to God again and family God replied, "I want you to humble yourself (**James 4:10**)." She said, OK. Lord!" Then as she rose from her knees, she thought about what that meant, *"Humble yourself?"*

Next, she began to think that maybe God wanted her to take a lesser appealing job just to see if she could and would, so she did or at least tried. Jasmine began to apply for employment at fast food restaurants, department stores, and anywhere else she saw a *"For Hire"* sign. Still she had no success. Jasmine's frustration grew with every rejection and every silent response. She did not know what to do.

Weeks had gone by and still no success. Her home front situation wasn't getting any better either. It was a battlefield. She felt surrounded by the enemy. Looking at her circumstances, (which we should never do) Jasmine cried out again- "Lord are you hearing me? I have bills to pay. I need food to eat. What am I doing wrong?

God replied.

"I want you to humble yourself!"

"Not again" she thought.

Now, don't you just detest that? Here you are trying to figure out the meaning behind someone else's thoughts with little to no clue as to what they mean. Now it would not be so bad if this person was a natural man, but this was God. His thoughts are higher than ours. Man has a hard enough time trying to figure out natural things, needless to say spiritual things. I sympathize with her because I know exactly how she feels.

Now, some of you *more mature folks* can probably see several of the mistakes that Jasmine made, but let us not lose site that this was a beginners training course and that Jasmine was not the only one in training. So were many of those around her too! Looking back over my trials, I can think of a few of that thought they were mature, but were in need of some additional training courses themselves too.

Humble Yourself!
Humble Yourself!

What did that mean? This statement that God was making was puzzling to her. Jasmine did not know what to think anymore. What could God mean by "*Humble yourself*?"

She looked in a dictionary for the meaning of humble. Little help did that do so Jasmine began to think harder as to what God meant. How much lower could she go? She thought that God was trying to be funny or something. To Jasmine, she thought that this was not a good time for God to be making jokes about her life right now. Despite of it all, it did not stop her from thinking even harder about what He meant. One day, Jasmine's, thoughts even led her to apply for help at the Department of Social Services. Three Times! They denied her each time.

Times were getting tougher and tougher for her and her family. They were barely making it. She tried to borrow from her family, but the headache they were putting her through was too much. It made her not want to ask, but she had kids to feed and bills to pay. She just could not figure out what God wanted her to do.

How many of you have been there? You are trusting God, but you are not sure of the next move that He wants you to make. This can be quite frustrating to those who are babes in Christ as well as some of us mature Christians too. However, the peace that God said that He would give had not yet been developed in her life, so Jasmine worried quite a bit.

At this point, Jasmine was at her wits end. Jasmine decided to make her final cry of desperation to the Lord.

She cried out-

"My God, What do you want me to do? What do you mean by "Humble yourself?" I just do not understand."

Then she fell down on her knees in tears: she wept for hours. Still, God said nothing.

Isn't that just like God? Those of you who have walked with the Lord through your own difficulties know that God can get silent. He got silent that day, over 2000 years ago, when His Son hung from the bark of a tree for the sins of you and me. Sometimes we feel that God has forgotten us and that we are walking alone, but word has it that it is in times like these God is carrying you right on through. That He is working behind the scenes on your behalf, you just don't know it yet!

With feelings of discouragement and despair, Jasmine pressed about her day doing what she could do around the house, trying to fill her thoughts with work so that she did not have to think about what was going on in her life.

Later that same evening, as she placed each child in their bed, God called unto her spirit.

He said,

"Jasmine, I have heard your cry and I have seen your tears.

I know that you have needs, and I know what you stand in need of. I want you to humble yourself to the point that you put your trust completely in me to provide just what you need. Not your husband, not your family or your friends, not a job or a government system, just *Me*."

God continued,

"You will be like the Israelites in the wilderness. Every day they waited and trusted Me to supply their needs and every day you will trust Me to supply what you need just the same. You will be in covenant with me and I will be in covenant with you. Then you will know that I am truly your God, Jehovah-Jireh, your provider."

Jasmine just fell to the floor and began to worship God in her pool of tears. Later on she began to think about the things God had said to her, Jasmine felt a sense of nervousness. She wasn't nervous about what God had said, but she was apprehensive about this unfamiliar journey that she was about to embark.

She had never been without before. She had always managed to work to provide what she needed. Now, she had to trust god, a God that she was still unfamiliar with, especially at this stage of her life.

Trusting God, at first, was not an easy thing for her to do. Jasmine began to understand why the Israelites murmured and complained in the wilderness. She was beginning to feel the same way. It was hard for her to forget about everything she knew concerning this natural life and the methods used for survival. Yet, she knew that she had no choice. This was the way God wanted it to be, and that was that. God wasn't having it any other way. Jasmine did not understand the importance of this trial that God placed her in, but she would soon find out.

Isn't that just like God? He had shut all of Jasmine's doors so that she would trust Him. He waited until she was desperate, with no way out, so that she would cry out to Him. Just like when God tested Job, Jasmine had to wait until her *change* came.

Now, why would God wait? I have come to know and learn, over a period of time, that if there is a natural way out of a situation, where we would not give God the glory, then God is not at the helm.

On the other hand God, comes in when it seems like all hope is gone and when it looks like you just cannot win. This way you cannot take the glory for yourself and give it to someone else. This way you will know that He is God. Jasmine, who in her process was trying to figure out what God meant by *humble yourself*, attempted to try to solve her problem through natural means which wasn't in the plan of what God wanted for this situation.

Jasmine was walking a *faith walk* which she was about to discover.

Faith is the substance of things hoped for.
The evidence of thing not seen.
The just shall live by faith!

Hebrew 11:1

I believe that many times we intervene with some of the miracles God wants to do in our lives by trying to solve them in a natural ways or the only way we know how.

I am not saying that God will not use natural means to solve our problems, but I am talking about us trying to fix problems ourselves and not allowing God to fix them. To wait, especially on God, requires patience. God has a way of taking your faith and your patience to a whole new level. Now, some of you are probably shaking your heads because you know exactly what I mean while others may feel different.

I once has a conversation with a close associate of mine who wanted money to get a bill paid. She did the normal thing, call family members to see if she could get the money from one of them. When she made these attempts, she got mad at those who would not help her for whatever the reason was. She eventually got the money but also made for herself some enemies in her family members.

When she told me this story, the Holy Spirit used me to tell her that she had no right to be mad at those who would not help her. Often times we run to people expecting them to be a source for us and when they disappoint us, we get mad at them. Well God told her that she was wrong.

Why?

Because she made her family her source and not Him. See when God promises to provide, He will, but then we get involved and try to give God a hand by trying to jump start the process. She decided to call her family instead of allowing God to choose the source. He decides who he wants to use to be a blessing to you. He could use your family, but he may not choose too for this matter. He may use a neighbor, a co-worker, a church member, a raven, or a donkey. The only thing God wants us to do is believe He will provide and then He will guide us through the rest of the process. Sure God will use man, but which man is up to God not for us to find the needle in the hay stack.

Back to the story

Well, this blew Jasmine's mind. Jasmine reread the story to recall the exact reasons why the Israelites stayed in the wilderness for so long. If most of you know the story about the Israelites in the wilderness, then you also know that they wandered there for forty (40) years (**Exodus 15:22-27 and 16:1-35**). Just the thought made Jasmine feel a tad-bit more discouraged. She wondered if God was going to make her go through this situation for forty years like the Israelites. She knew that they wandered for forty years because of their murmuring and complaining, and she did not want to stay in this position any longer than necessary. To guarantee this, she said that she would try to do her best not to murmur or complain. Remember, what I just said, she did her best, and we know how our best can be sometimes.

Jasmine became perplexed by this situation. This was unfamiliar territory to her. She was on a trip to a foreign place that she knew that she had no choice but to go through. She thought about how this experience invited itself upon her.

Later, that next day, the Holy Spirit helped her to recall a conversation that she had with God in California, when this trial had emerged. In California, Jasmine asked God to teach her and train her so that she could fight for him. Believe me, God took that covenant very seriously. I can recall situations in my own life when I asked god to give me patience. Boy I will never do that again. When you ask for patience, you ask for trials that involve you being patient. Remember, be careful what you ask for because you just might get it.

Trusting God

A new city, a new home, with feelings of abandonment from her husband and her family, Jasmine could not help feeling that her life was that of Jobs. Trusting God was not easy for her to do, especially coming from a past where trusting someone was not something that she was good at.
It was hard for her to trust people; therefore, she had a hard time trusting God. Believe me when I say Jasmine struggled through this lesson.

There is so much more that she could say about her trial, but it is not the details of every event that took place that God wants you to know; it is what she learned from them.

God was now the Potter and Jasmine was His clay. He began His work in shaping and molding her into God's Woman.

"Then I went down to the potter's house and behold, he wrought a work on the wheels. And the vessel that he made of clay was marred in the hand of the potter; so he made it again another vessel, as seemed good to the potter to make it. Then the word of the Lord came to me saying, O house of Israel, cannot I do with you as the potter? saith the Lord. Behold as the clay is in the potter's hand, so are ye in mine hand, O house of Israel. "
Jeremiah 18:3-6

Chapter 3

FROM ISOLATION TO REVELATION

With the temporary loss of employment, a wayward husband, and soon to be four children, things were tight. Food was now at an all-time low. The children were growing and they needed everything, so Jasmine prayed as God instructed her. Then she prayed some more and prayed again.

As Jasmine began praying on her knees morning, noon, and night, God showed up and supplied her with what she needed just as He said He would. Now this did not come without a price. Jasmine had to learn to be patient and wait on God to get her what she needed. Waiting can be a kicker in itself, especially if you are not a patient person. Naturally, she waited. God supplied her family with exactly what they needed for that day and not a bit more.

God seemed to have placed Jasmine in a period of

isolation from the world. She had no friends whom to talk. She had no means of transportation back and forth to find a church because she had to depend upon her husband to take her around. Unfortunately, he was like a swinging pendulum most of the time. Some days he acted like her husband, and other days he acted like her enemy.

At first when they arrived to Maryland, neither of them had a job, and a life between them was normal. Eventually, he found a job, and that's when everything changed again. His working was not always beneficial to them. He used the job to benefit himself, but not her. Every now and then it seemed that he would take pity on the family and give them some money and take them shopping for food. Of course, that was only as God moved upon his heart. He was cold and harsh towards her. It was as if he saw her as his enemy. Jasmine had to battle with him every day too. Looking at someone you love and not having them love you back can be a hurting thing to go through on top of everything else you are facing.

Who was this man she married? Where did the real one go? It was hard to believe that this was her husband. The man who stood before God and vowed to love, honor, and cherish, the father of her kids. It saddened her heart sometimes just to look at him.

Just thinking about him made her wonder how he could hate her so much. She tried everything not to think about negative things like that and to stay focused on God. She knew that once she took her eyes off of God those negative feelings would surface again leaving her sad, depressed, and filled with despair. Plus in California she learned that her battles were not battles of the flesh, but of the spirit (**Ephesians 6:10-18**). Reacting in the flesh will prove to be very ineffective when fighting a spiritual battle.

So, Jasmine tried hard not to look at him. In this process of getting to know God for herself, she was learning that God was greater than any problem that she could have or ever face. However, it was a lesson learned with a price.

Every now and then God would soften her sister's heart, and she would stop by with a few things for them to eat, but even her sister's selfishness bothered Jasmine at times. Not that they had the greatest relationship to begin with, but they were sisters. Blood that is supposed to be thicker than water. Theirs was proving to be quite thin at this moment. Right before her eyes, Jasmine saw the people who she loved most in her life become weapons that her adversary used against her. First her husband, now her sister. Little did they know that no weapon formed against her would prosper (**Isaiah 54:17**)? Little did jasmine know either?

Jasmine would have never imagined her own sister would taunt her so, especially in her time of need. But it was happening. Everyone that she thought would be there for her was not. It had become plain to see that she and God were alone. On the brighter side of things, Jasmine saw how God was providing her family with what they needed. Not in the abundance that she had grown accustom, but they ate, they had shelter, and clothes on their backs. God was meeting their needs.

It was during moments like those that Jasmine observed the mighty hand of the Lord at work in her life. He use mankind to bless them even when they did not want to be a blessing. God's power was at work in Jasmine's life and she marveled at the things that He was doing. Spiritually, Jasmine was feeling stronger, but her flesh was hurting badly.

Let me stop here for a moment. I can really identify with Jasmine. Dying to the flesh is not always easy to do. It can be quite painful to your ego, your pride, and your emotions. Submitting yourself means to give up the old program of life, the one you thought was right, to learn a whole new program.

Many temptations arose with an opportunity for her to do wrong in order to make ends meet. Her flesh was squirming to find out, but the spirit was standing strong in convicting her of any thought to do wrong. Jasmine was growing up spiritually. She was coming to the place where she could not see herself apart from God. It was just her and God alone. He became her best friend.

This may sound a little strange to most, but she would tell jokes to God, read the Bible with Him in bed, and they would watch TV together. She began to fall in love with God, and she could not imagine life without Him. God was her husband, her friend, her father, and anyone she needed Him to be (**Jeremiah 31:32 and Psalm 68:5**).

No, she wasn't crazy because she knew that this is what God wants our relationship with Him to be. We should all reach this place where we fall in love with God-Where nothing else matters, but Him.

The Word of God tells us to "Acknowledge Him in all of our ways and He will direct our path," and Jasmine took that seriously. With every thought, with every action, God became her focus and her drive. She wanted to know what He thought, with every action, God became her focus and her drive. She wanted to know what He thought about everything that she did and thought about doing. This is what God wants us to do. Put Him FIRST! When He says to acknowledge Him in all our ways, what does the word ALL mean? It means EVERYTHING!

There is nothing that concerns you that does not concern God. Your hair, your health, your outfit for the day, and even the most minute things, God cares about them. Yet, we do not think that He does. God is waiting for us to include Him. It is up to us to do so. God will only come in when we invite Him in. He will only go as far as we want Him. The Holy Spirit is God's active force. The Spirit doesn't force himself upon us. The Spirit waits until we invite God in, and most times that's when we have screwed up things so badly that only God can bring us out. It should not be that way, but it is for most of us.

"Trust in the Lord with all your heart and lean not on your own understanding; in all your ways acknowledge him, and he will make your paths straight."
Proverbs 3:5-6

I do not know why we do things backwards, but I have done the same thing. Backwards! Here we have a loving God who wants so much to be a part of our lives. He wants nothing but our good, yet we think apart from Him we can do anything and everything. I hate to give some of you this rude awakening, but apart from God you can do nothing (John 15:5). That is why we eventually mess things up. Look at the world now. It is messed up because sin destroys. Sin rips out the core of a society and leaves it destitute, colds and heartless, even though society may think it is not.

Just think about how our lives would be if God was at the helm of everything we did from the very beginning. It would be like heaven on earth. If we placed His ways and His will power will over our own wicked and evil ways, everything that concerns us would be cared for. Oh! What a life that would be, but in most cases, He is not.

Time went on and God's faithfulness to His word He fulfilled. One day a door opened. A door to the outside world in the form of – A Friend! God once again blessed Jasmine with someone to whom she could socialize. She and her new friend, Janet, actually met because of Jasmine's husband.

Apparently, Jasmine's husbands waywardness

found himself friends with Janet's brother who happened to think that Jasmine and his sister should meet and they did. Jasmine's new friendship with Janet began with four months of phone conversations because neither of them drove. Never setting eyes upon each other, it felt like Jasmine and Janet knew each other for a lifetime. Before long Jasmine and Janet's friendship grew and they began feeling more like sisters. They felt spiritually connected from birth. Finally, one day they met and it made their friendship blossom even more, but God did not stop there.

Not too long after that, some new neighbors moved in across the street from where Jasmine and her family lived and God led Jasmine right to them. They too became friends. Occasionally, Jasmine, her two neighbors, and her husband would hold prayer together. In those moments their new neighbor's husband would try to help Jasmine's husband get his life together. The neighbors tried to minister to his problems, but it was still up to Jasmine's husband to put God's Word into effect in his life. He listened at times, but he still made excuses for his actions.

Therefore, his changes lasted for a short period of time.

The Lessons

Now there are two lessons in this: First, we must be willing to help people, but they must also be willing to help themselves too. We cannot be expected to do the work that they need to do for themselves. Our elders had a saying that reminds me of situations like this and that is, "You can bring a horse to the water, but you cannot make them drink it." Many of us get frustrated with family, friends, and love ones who God has given us to help but they are not willing to make those changes necessary for their lives, so we try to make those changes for them. If must understand that, they must be willing to make those changes, otherwise no change will come. We should not get frustrated with them.

Why? Because God says that we play one of two parts in a person's life. We either plant or water. God knows how lone the planting season will last and how much water is needed. These are our two lanes and we need to learn to stay in them.

God said it is He who brings the increase. So in that appointed time increase or harvest comes and we see, if He allows it, what was growing all along. Remember, Man's desire to act a particular way is the key factor to whether or not they will surrender all of their desires to God. We must submit our will to God in order to grow in Him. Just think where you are struggling right now!

The second lesson is: there are many of us that God has graciously extended an abundance of mercy and grace because of those fervent prayers of the righteous so that we can make those necessary changes in our lives. God has sent people to help us. In return, we reject them and their help because we are not willing to change. We must understand that our rejection of them is our rejection of God. It is His Word that they refuse to accept, not ours so do not fret. God told us what to do when we are not received by others in **Luke 10:10**, so read it.

Not only did the friendships bring about an opportunity for Jasmine's husband to have godly counsel, but the church that her new neighbors attended had a van service that picked up people who did not have transportation; as a result, off to church Jasmine and her family went! Door 2 opens.

The doors around Jasmine were finally beginning to open slightly. She still had no success finding a job. Bills were still piling-up, but the family still ate every day. They still had clean clothes to wear, a roof over their heads, and now to top it off, God had gave them some true godly friends and a church to attend. Life could not have been any better right then for Jasmine. She appreciated God for all the things that He was doing in her life. She was learning to be satisfied where God had placed her. Everything that was in that house was a gift from God: the couch she sat on, the bed she slept on, and the table she ate at, but that's another story by itself. God was truly Jehovah-Jireh her provider.

Apostle Paul tells us in Philippians 4:12-to be content in whatever the circumstances may be. We should know how to live with things and how to live without them. This is difficult for many because we are a materialistic world and unfortunately many of God's children still carry that spirit into the church and stay with it. This is why we have so many pilfering the sheep now.

While Jasmine did appreciated the friends God had given her, she had also become comfortable with just being alone with God. The relationship between them was all she felt she ever needed. This isolation period had trained her to trust and put God first every time a problem occurred to get some help and not seek someone else for her provision or encouragement. When the friends came, Jasmine understood the direct order of God's communication. God first and that's the way it is!

Don't misunderstand Jasmine. She knew that God could only use anyone to accomplish just about anything He wanted to do. She was seeing Him work right before her very eyes. As a matter of fact, the house that she lived in was run by a natural man, however even without the money to pay the rent, God was able to touch his heart to allow her to stay with no money at all. Not for one month, but for over a year. But God! Only God can do that! If she had tried to fix it, who knows what might have happened and gone wrong.

The difference in the two lessons is we must allow God to make the moves and not use our methods to make them. A lot of times we try to fix our own problems instead of letting God fight our battles for us (**2 Chronicles 32:8**).

At some point in our lifetimes, we have all tried to get others we know to help us get better seat at a show or to help us get a jump on just about anything. I believe the term is called *hook up* or *networking*. Well, God is our heavenly *hookup* because He works out all the situations that we choose to let Him work out for us. God is our network system. By cooperating with God through obedience we get all kinds of connections from Heaven. We call on God no matter what time of day or night, and He answers. All we have to do is leave it in His hands, and it's as good as done (**Peter 5:7**).

In our own strength we will not be able to open up the appropriate doors that are needed for us to achieve God's goal: to get that job, that husband, or whatever is we have need of. Only God holds the key to success, life with abundance, and death. He is the landlord who holds the key to the world and all that it contains.

So why do we look to do things ourselves? Well, it is because we are conditioned from birth to be independent, however our relationship with God is based upon dependency. Therefore, we struggle to get back to the original order of things.

Let's look at Adam and Eve in the Garden of Eden. God provided Adam with everything that he could need: a wife, a job, a place to live (which was beautiful), and food. All needs met. God also gave them a choice: the tree of the knowledge of good and evil or the tree of life, but they partook of the tree of the knowledge of good and evil. Man's first opportunity to choose the direction for their lives, and they chose wrong (Genesis 2-3). So do many of us.

God began to move Jasmine out into the world of people. He lifted the period of isolation and used her to minister to others in areas of her growth. One day while Jasmine was in prayer in her secret place, the Lord God asked her to go downstairs and speak to the young lady next door. Jasmine said,

"Lord, What do I say?"

He said, "Take no thoughts as to what you will say because at the appointed time the Spirit will give it to you.

> *"For the Holy Spirit will teach in that hour what you ought to say."*
> *Luke 12:12*

If you did not know, then let me be the first to say, "God will use you right in the midst of your storm to bless and help others." His principles of reaping and sowing does not pertain only to the high places in our lives- When the money is good and all is well, but He will also use you when money is low and all is not well. It is in our valley experiences that we should *give* more because God wants to get more to us, so we plant for our future. Just make sure that you are sowing in good ground.

> *"Whatever a man sows; sow shall he also reap"*
> *Galatians 6:7*

Well, Jasmine went downstairs and peeked out of the door. The girl God had spoken about was sitting there. Her mind was racing fast about what to say. She took an extra walk around the corner. When she came back, Jasmine sat on her steps. Finally, she said "Nice weather we are having, isn't it." The weather outside was hot. The girl replied- "Yes." Then, Jasmine kept on talking about the hot weather that they were having lately. From the conversation, Jasmine could feel that something was bothering the girl, but she did not want to press too hard. Sometimes, we just need to let things take its natural spiritual course.

Eventually, the conversation led to the topic about church. How? Jasmine could not recall, but it did. Jasmine asked the girl if she went to church, and in her response the truth of her hurt surfaced. Later, she became so comfortable with Jasmine that she began to talk about how she had been hurt by her previous church, some of the folks that attended there, and how life for her was hard enough right now.

Tell me about it!

I know many of you are saying the same thing. We all go through some hard places.

Moments when we have and moments when we don't, but it upsets me to hear about the experiences this young lady is having. Jasmine doesn't want those details exposed, but I can say that we must become more sensitive to our new Sisters and Brothers in Christ. Sometimes we expect too much from them and think that they should grow overnight. They have a lot of misconceptions and wrong perceptions. Mature Christians must be mindful of their ways so that their mannerisms and behaviors do not deter nor chase people away.

Well, Jasmine and this young lady talked for hours about her life. Everyday this young lady would stop by to talk. Finally, Jasmine invited her to their new church home where she surrendered her life. They went together every Sunday. Every now and then Jasmine's husband would go too. That was a blessing. Although some good things were happening for them, her life was still totally dependent upon the Lord. At this point, things looked as if they were getting better and they were.

Remember, it was still not the life-style that Jasmine and her family were accustomed too, but it was better than the wilderness that they were in. I guess sometimes we have to lose some things in order to appreciate them once we get them again.

I am going to stop again because it is important for the true Christians to understand that during our trials and tests there will be times when we have to let go of some of our earthly possessions. Remember Job? Job lost a whole lot. He lost most of his possessions as well as his loves ones. All that Job lost, yet, he did not curse God. Although we may lose our possessions in the course of tests, God is faithful because nothing that is lost remains lost forever. As you may already know, Job's latter blessings were greater than what he had before. God promises to restore the years that the caterpillar, cankerworm and locust have eaten (**Joel 2:25**). What God have done for others, he is able to do for you.

Jasmine still did not have a job nor the means to support her family. Her husband, although trying to behave and put forth an effort to be obedient to God, was still disappearing on them and still very unstable. The church that Jasmine attended was a nice church. People were friendly, but they could see that there were things going on in her life between her and her husband. Jasmine's husband, during his obedient stages, actually talked with the pastor about some of the things he was going through. The pastor would talk with him during the times he did attend and even called the house on several occasions to talk with him, but it only helped for a very short moment. Shortly after the sessions, he was off again.

Up to this point, we have talked about all the fruits that were manifested because of Jasmine's willingness to submit her life into the hands of almighty God. Well, it was not all roses. Jasmine had many weak moments: Moments when she felt like giving up and walking away. Moments when she was angry with God because things did not always go the way she thought they should. This walk with God is not an easy one, especially if you want to be in His perfect will.

There will be many things that you must do even when you don't want to do them. There will be many times when you do not understand why things are happening the way they do. Moments when you must bear all things. Moments when you feel alone, as if God does not care or hear you. I know how Jasmine felt as many of you may know too.

Let's go back to the story!

Still none of this helped the fact that she had not paid rent for several months, that food was scarce, and that clothes and shoes were needed for everyone in the family, except her husband. Nevertheless, Jasmine still trusted in God. Although she was beginning to feel tired of not having for her kids, sometimes Jasmine had to ask her family. They rejected and/or humiliated her. Watching her husband rip and run out of their lives with very little concern for their welfare was leading Jasmine to think that life was just unfair. Every time she thought about complaining, she thought about spending forty years in the wilderness.

A story that was embedded in her spirit. With determination, she tried to keep her mouth shut, but that was hard to do because she was such an outspoken person.

People saw Jasmine going through and wondered how she kept her joy. She was always kind to others and helpful to those who needed her. She never complained, at least not to them. She walked with her head held high as if she did not have a care in the world. Jasmine tried to hide the tiredness that was burdening her. She refused to let the Devil get any joy out of her pain and suffering. Inside, alone with God, is where she released all of those feelings of hurt, rejection, abandonment, disappointment, sorrow, and pain. It was during those times that God comforted her and gave her strength to fight on. People just did not now that it was not easy.

This is an important fact for the true Christians to understand. We should never present ourselves in an unkept state or go around boasting about what we are going through. We should learn to suffer in silence no matter what we are going through, and we should look clean and fresh every day. Sometimes we want everyone to know what we are facing and even want to dress the part too. Looking for Man to see how much we bear for Christ. I know this to be true because I have seen it happen. People who look depressed all day and won't take care of themselves. Know that God will place people in our lives to comfort us and exhort us during these moments. We do not have to place ourselves out there to find them. Now, lets' go back to the story!

It wasn't that Jasmine was at all ungrateful for what God was doing in her life. For she could have gone without and not worry, but it was her children's needs that began to wear her down the most: Not being able to get the children the things that they saw her family nieces and nephews with. Not being able to send them on school trips. All of this is what really bothered her most, yet she refused to let go of who God was to her and who she knew He could be. She took the Word of God for its truth. Truths that could not lie. So, she hung in there: Praying most of the day and most of the night. Crying out to the Lord for the things her children needed.

Crying out for the deliverance of her household. *Just crying!*

One day while in prayer, God asked Jasmine- "Who is thy neighbor?" She was not sure how to reply, so she asked, "Which one Lord. The one on the right or the one on the left." He said, "Both of them and many more." Then He instructed her to reread the story about the Good Samaritan and she did after realizing her memory of it was not going to work. She read it several times before she realized why God had required her to read this parable again. It paralleled her life. God showed her that she was the certain man, in the parable, that came from one town (California) to another (Maryland), who got stripped of everything (husband, possessions, finances, job) and was wounded, left for death (eviction, starvation, spiritually). They were wounds that could leave her naturally as well as spiritually dead. God showed her that many of the people that interacted with her on a daily basis were the priest and Levites of her life, but Oh, who were those Good Samaritans?

It was during this period in Jasmine's life that God wanted to build her faith. He wanted her to learn more about the heart of God, His ways, and to test the hearts of others around her. Was this her test alone? No! Many were involved. They just didn't know that they were being tested!

Those who hope in the Lord will renew their strength. They will soar on wings like eagles; they will run and not grow weary, they will walk and not be faint.
Isaiah 40:31

The Good Samaritan Remix

Traveler- anyone; man in his fallen state
The Robbers- world; Satan
The Priest/Levites- the church; legalism
The Samaritan- Jesus, Redeemed Man

There is another possible way to interpret the Parable of the Good Samaritan, and that is as a metaphor. In this interpretation the injured man is all men in their fallen condition of sin. The robbers are Satan and his demons attacking man with the intent of destroying their relationship with God. The lawyer is mankind without the true understanding of God and His Word. Jesus told us that the beginning of wisdom began with getting God's understanding which the religious scholars of that time did not. They made their own interpretation of what they thought God meant.

The priest is religion in an apostate condition. In other words it is Christianity being rejected by someone who was formerly a Christian. Those in this condition cannot see or recognize that they are. It's the example of the false church system. A church without faith and that relies on its own knowledge and strength.

The Levite is legalism that instills prejudice into the hearts of believers. Basically legalism is any doctrine which states salvation comes strictly from adherence to the law. It can be thought of as a works=based religion. Its rules and regulation that one must follow that have been set by man. It is motivated by self-ambition.

The Samaritan is Jesus who provides the way to spiritual health. Samaritan's were despised and rejected by the Jews. Jesus was despised and rejected by mankind (Isaiah 53:3). However, it is through the despised one, Jesus that all must come to be saved. According to the parable of the Good Samaritan, the Samaritan gave him first aid, cleaned his wounds, provide his need and paid the cost for all that he would need. Sounds familair1. It should because Jesus does the same for us and a whole lot more? It's a story of love, redemption, and salvation rolled up in one.

Although this interpretation teaches good lessons, and the parallels between Jesus and the Samaritan are striking, this understanding draws attention to Jesus that does not appear to be intended in the text.

Therefore, we must conclude that the teaching of the Parable of the Good Samaritan is simply a lesson on what it means to love one's neighbor. In love there is mercy by which we are supposed to demonstrate to all. Blessed are those who show mercy for mercy will be upon them. Who doesn't need mercy?

Chapter 4

THE HEART OF THE MATTER!

Now we have come to the heart of the mater. This is where we can either lose the chains that bind our hearts or we can remain chained and in bondage. As Christians we must be willing to seek the truth in order to free our hearts and minds from matters that have us bound.

As stated in the previous chapter, many of us have been excluded from the truth concerning the parable of the Good Samaritan. Some see parables as stories that are told just to children in the form of fairy tales (**2 Timothy 4:3-5**).

Others may see them as stories not relevant to our present day. Jesus used parables to illustrate and provide wisdom to His disciples and those that followed along the journey.

Just reading the surface of these parables will not give us all the truth and wisdom that they contain. We must study and ask God to give us the wisdom of Christ in order that we might see and understand those hidden truths.

We are considered servants of the Lord and as servants we do thing: SERVE! (**1 Cor. 4:1**) Who do we get a choice in whom we want to serve, especially if we want to obey God? If you were an owner of a business and asked one of your employees to go here or there, would you not expect them to do exactly what you said? Suppose your employee decided that he/she did not want to help a certain customer that you deemed valuable. Would you not accept him/her to service them anyhow? Well, it is no different with God. God's Word is the policy that we must follow. His Word gives us requirements for even being hired. To remain employed, we must follow the rules and regulations that govern His world.

Simon, Peter faced this in **Acts 10:1-39** when God gave him a vision that opened the way for the Gentiles.

Peter doubted in himself what this vision, which he saw, should mean, but he was obedient.

The lesson is: God is not always going to lead us to people we are familiar or comfortable with. We will do things that will go against what others may not understand as of yet. Many of us go to work and even work hard on our natural jobs to receive raises and promotions. Again, God is no different because He gives to each of us according to the faith that works in us.

What does this mean?

This means that we need to apply ourselves and work just as hard for the kingdom of God as we do on our natural jobs so that others will see God in us, with us, and through us. Really this is all that matters. We give and sacrifice, not for the recognition form Man, but so that Man might see God's love for them through us.

If we do it for any other reason, then we do it to become pleasers of men and our reward is the recognition we receive from them (**Matthew 6:1-2**).

As Christians we tend to think that the options offered in life are the same options that we have in service to God's Kingdom. God has only given mankind two options for living in this life. An option to be obedient or disobedient. An option to serve or not to serve (**Luke 16:13**), but if you choose to serve God, you must serve Him with gladness (Psalm 100:2) and the Father will honor them who serve Him because where He is, there will His servant be also (**John 12:26**).

Deuteronomy 11:13-16 says, *"And it shall be that if you earnestly obey my commandments which I command you today, to love the Lord God and serve Him with all your heart and with all your soul then I will give you the rain fir your land in its season, the early rain and latter rain that you may gather in your grain, your new wine and your oil."* These are the blessings of true Servant hood to the Almighty God, but there are consequences as well, **Deuteronomy 11:16-17** goes on to say, *"Take heed to yourselves llest your heart be deceived, and you turn aside and serve other gods and worship them."*

As a consequence, *"The Lord's anger will arouse against you and he will shut up the heavens so that there be no rain and the land yield no produce, and you perish quickly from the good land which the Lord is giving you."* In other words, if you want to receive the promise of wealth and prosperity, the good life that God has for His people, the riches that are laid up for the just, health and long life then you will do as the Word tells you to do without justification and without rationalization, but rightly dividing the Word of Truth (**2Timothy 2:15**) because you love Him, submission and services is easier for us to do.

The Word says that if we love God, we will obey Him (**Johns 14:15**). Our relationship with God is like a marriage. When we are saved, our surrendering comes with the promise form us to love, honor, cherish and obey Him, whether we are with sickness or in good health. In other words, through the good times and the bad times, we should forsake all others and cleave only to Him, not putting anything or anyone before Him. So, "What shall separate us from the love of God (**Romans 8:35**)?"

Unfortunately, there is another illness that affects our walk with Christ. This illness that I am referring to is not our everyday natural sickness like a cold or a disease. I am talking about a spiritual sickness of sin- Our minds are poisoned by false doctrines, ungodly traditions, and beliefs. These are empty things which cannot profit or deliver us for they are nothing, but lies that separate us from the love of God.

Yet, slowly we allow these empty things to creep into our minds causing us to become confused and led away by the wind. Before we know it, we are outside of the will of God. Sick from false truths, we will need to be restored back to good health. Good health is the healing that begins when we either accept Christ into our lives for the first time or when we rededicate ourselves to him once again. To stay healthy we must not engage ourselves in those things that once separated or drove us away.

We must value the price that was paid over 2000 years ago and because we do not, we stray away most times without fear.

God tells us to serve the Lord with fear (**Psalm 2:11**). The fear of God is the beginning of knowledge (**Proverbs 1:7**). If we fear Him we will keep His commandments (**Deuteronomy 12:4**), but many of us have depreciated the price of Christ's life. On the wooden stake, Jesus took away our sins, bore our sickness, and all manners of diseases. On the cross, He defeated all of our adversaries that would rise up against us. For the price Christ paid, how can we be so selfish and unconcerned one to another?

For such a price, why do we feel that we can call ourselves children of God and then misrepresent, through our actions, God any which way we want? That is why God's Word tells us that we know a tree by the fruit that bears (**Matthew 7:16-20**). Good trees yield good fruit and bad trees yield bad fruit, so examine yourself to see what kind of fruit you are bearing.

God loves the sinner and the righteous ones, for the earth is the Lord's and the fullness thereof (**Cor. 10:26**). Unfortunately, we have sisters and brothers that are disobedient. Some that do not know their

Heavenly Father and others who do, but choose not to listen? Even in our natural families, we have siblings that don't always listen to their parents. Maybe it was you or one of the others, but our parents did not love us any less. If anything, it may have seems to some of us, but that was because our parents wanted them to succeed just like the rest. Read the Prodigal Son, **Luke 15:11-32**.

God's love is no different. It is not His wish that any should perish, but that all have eternal life (**2 Peter 3:9**). God extends His mercy and grace to them too. We were once disobedient, and if it were not for God's mercy and grace where would many of us be?

As their brothers and sisters, we need to love them into the kingdom. At no point should we accept their sinful conditions, but minister to them in hope that they too will be saved (1Corint. 5:11 & 2 Thessalonians 3:14-15). God's love for us covered a multitude of our sins and with this same love we must do the same (1 peter 4:8 & James 5:20).

In order for us to obtain this type of love, we must be willing to submit our will to God's will and His ways. This is a lot to swallow because submission is not easy for everyone. We become adults and forget that we are children in the sight of God. This is why God says to us:

"Except ye be converted, and become as little children, ye shall not enter into the kingdom of heaven."
Matthew 8:23

Even with our redemption after the crucifixion of Jesus, our rebirth starts us as babes in Christ (**1 Corinthians 3:1-3**). Christians who still have many traditions and ways of the world must renew their minds and through the submission of their wills' grow into maturity in Christ. In this process, God, our parent, rewards us for our good and chastens us when we do wrong (**Revelations 3:19**). His patience, mercy, and grace bring us to place where we begin to mature. As we begin grow-up, we let go of the milk and begin to digest the meat.

As mature children, with the meat of the Word, we can thereafter care for others who have not let go of the milk or those who just haven't been conceived yet. Why does God call us children if we are adults?

Well, a child is teachable and easier to humble. As adults we lose some sensitivity because life teaches us to be hard, less forgiving, and some of us quite cocky in our attitudes. Through submission and obedience to God's Word, we are reconditioned. We lose the edge that the world developed in us.

God also says that if a child does not obey his/her parents, his/her life will not go well, and that his/her days on this earth will be shorten (**Ephesians 6:1-3**).

Many of us teach this scripture to our natural children, yet we do not realize that the same verse applies to us in relationship to God. If we are not obedient as children of God, our lives are affected just the same. There are many scriptures, approximately 1772 verses that deal with God calling us children.

We are adults only on earth to our children, but not in the sight of God. If we get anything from this Word let us, above all things receive understanding **(Proverbs 4:7).**

How does all of this relate to the parable of the Good Samaritan in relationship to Jasmine's life? If you read Luke 10:37, God said that we should go and do the same as the Good Samaritan. Did the Samaritan know the man he helped? No. This man was on his way to a new land. The reason is irrelevant. He was wounded and he needed help. Those who should have known better did absolutely nothing for him; they looked passed by the other side at that. They turned and walked away from someone who was dying. Most of us do this every day. You know them.

They are the ones that dodge people because they are afraid they that they might ask them for something especially MONEY! The love of money-which is evil. When the parable talks about the man being wounded, it doesn't just specify a physical cut or bruise, although it is safe for us to say that it does.

Needless to say, often time we are sometimes wounded emotionally, spiritually, and financially. Being left for dead which does not necessarily mean just a physical death, but also a spiritual one. If a person is not redeemed they are spiritually dead, and those of us who know Christ, but remains carnal minded, are paralyzed.

"Let no one seek his own, but each one the other's well being."
1 Corinthians 10:24

Nevertheless, it is our responsibility to take care of others without being partakers of their sins. Most of us know this, yet we still don't do it. Maybe to a relative who we don't seem to care about or to a person who is always talking about their problems or to a friend who's in need- Either one, we have dodged them. WHY? We begin to rationalize the truth we know. Once we rationalize, we begin to decide on who we want to serve. We harden our hearts to some and just turn and walk away from others. We pretend that we do not see.

I was convicted of this same crime.

For example, there were times when I had hoped that the light would turn green so that the man begging, at the light, could not ask me for anything. Or when I saw the friend who always wants to talk about her problems, I walked the other way. Yes, I was no different than most of you. Sometimes, we have to go through those very things to regain our sensitivity to others.

What is amazing is in the midst of our disobedience, at being Good Samaritans, we cry "Lord God bless me." For what? So that we can buy more material things and still not be willing to bless others. We are blessed so that we can be a blessing (**Gen. 12:2**). Along with being a blessing, God commands us to love our enemies, do good to those who hat us, bless those who curse us, and pray for those who spitefully use us (**Luke 6:27-28**).

We love them despite their actions and are givers to everyone who ask us (**Matthews 5:42**). We do this hoping for nothing in return, then our reward will be great- We will be sons and daughters of the Most High.

God is always kind to His children including the unthankful and the evil (**Luke 6:30.35**).

Think about it! Hasn't God treated you this way many times before? Let's see! He did it when we were yet sinners, He sent His son to die for us. He did it when we were hardhearted and disobedient and when we made a mess of things. Nevertheless, He delivered us anyhow. How dare we take the same mercy and grace that God has shown to us, and refuse to give it to others. I hear people say all the time-

"Well, I am not God."

Although that is true, we are the children of God and He has placed in us His Holy Spirit the active force that works through us that we can be all that He is- Imitators of God and his Son. If we are the children of God, we have the same mind that is in Christ Jesus. With Christ's mind and our new heart, which He has so freely given to us, we have no excuse as to why we cannot do what is required of us.

Is there anything too hard for God (**Jeremiah 32:17**)? "No", then it is not too hard for us either! Through Christ we can do all things (**Philippians 4:13**).

Many of the tests that others face include us. Think about this?

Why had God allowed us to view or even hear the problems of another? What do you suppose God wanted us to know these things for? It is so that we can see how others suffer? Maybe it is so can see how holy they are going through?

No, I don't think so!

The truth is that God wants you to help them. If the disciples had walked away from everyone who they had come across, then many would not have been converted. The disciples ministered to any and every one. They even travelled to places where they heard that there was a need. While it may appear that Jasmine's only lesson from this trial was to trust Him and that she did, it was others whom God wanted to use to bless the Jasmines of this world? During the breakfast at the sea, after Jesus was resurrected, Jesus asked Simon Peter three times if he loved Him.

Each time, Simon answered "You know I do," and each time Jesus asked Simon to *"Feed His lambs, Tend His sheep and Feed His sheep* (**John 21:1-17**)." Who was God talking to when He said, "Feed my sheep?" He was talking to, His chosen people that's who, and many of us, including Jasmine, have failed to take care of God's people the way that we should yet; we expect God to take care of us and bless us with wealth.

Although this test is apparently Jasmine's, this test doesn't appear to be for you, but it is for you too. Our response to these matters are our test. This is where God tests our love and compassion for others, even our mercy and grace towards them. The test will tell you just how much of God's love abides in your heart.

Needless to say, Jasmine was beginning to find out who were really her neighbors!

God released Jasmine from her period of isolation to bring her more revelation than she could ever imagine. It wasn't just so that she could finally have some friends. It was for so much more. It was for a moment such as this. A message to be delivered to His people and to help set them on the right path. Jasmine had friends, family, and a neighborhood of people who knew her and yet she went without. Jasmine's survival was by the Almighty Hand of her gracious and loving God. God was not only teaching Jasmine patience, but also longsuffering, faith and love. He was also teaching her about His people. Those who call themselves His anointed, appointed, and chosen. It is during this trial that God identified the Levites and priests of this present day.

Anyone who came around Jasmine knew that things were not going well in her life. Granted, some knew more than others, but they knew. Even people in the neighborhood who did not know her well, knew. However, no one offered to baby-sit unless she asked, and some were reluctant to do that. Very few made the sacrifice of the cost of a meal to help her.

Many of the people that helped her were not her Christian brothers or sisters. Most of them were people who did not have that relationship with Christ. It should not have been. The Levite and the priest should have been the first ones to help her. Instead it took someone else to come along and do the job that God has told us to do. It is this behavior that saddens Christ. Many of us do this on a daily basis because we have just gotten so cold and hardhearted. I know some of you have been swindled by false preachers and deceptive Christians, but we cannot allow them to stop us from doing the work of God. That is why God tells us to pray for those who spitefully use us. He knew that we would come across those that would. Yet, there are those who are just stingy and selfish. We should pray for them daily.

God had used the unrighteous people in Jasmine's life to bless her, but when does the house take care of the house. If God chooses to use the unrighteous to bless Jasmine, that's good, but her brothers and sisters in the spirit should have looked out for her also.

The fact is that they should have been the first to help. Assistance from the unrighteous should have been just as added plus. God makes the unrighteous bless us, but He should not have to do that with the true Christians. When we come across matters or situations, we should ask god is there anything I can do to help them, but we don't. We just ignore or walk away with some hoping that they don't ask them.

Many of her Levite brothers and sisters offered prayer and prayer is good to do, but if after the prayer is over, and she is still hungry, then what? Do we just walk away, and she remains hungry still? This is a need not met.

Who is thy neighbor?

With all those people around Jasmine she should have had a steak meal every day, but she struggled to eat. There were days when she did not eat at all. Where were God's people? Oh yes, they were praying for her needs. They would say, "Girl, God is going to bless you," and they went on their way.

They would say, "Lord fill her cabinets," and still they would walk away. She knew in her heart that they meant well, but their good intentions did not satisfy the need. Neither did the intentions of the priest or Levite who just looked upon the man and passed by on the other side. He was still there wounded and left to die.

We have people in our churched who are not strong and they are barely hanging on. They just need someone to show them that they care, and that could make all the difference in their life. Yet, many go unattended too. Their needs totally not met. There are communities' right here that need food and clothing, yet many have not.

Why?

Our own selfish need to gain more and more for our personal pleasures. Meanwhile, we *give* very little in return. What is one less trip to the all you can eat buffets? It's a meal for someone else.

It is not the sole responsibility of the pastor to care for the flock; it is ours too. This is why so many leave the church wounded and go back into the world because they do not see the difference between the world and church. They should. We need to let the world see the difference between them and us. People like Jasmine can be ignored in the world and sometimes are, but when they come to the House of the Lord, they should find peace, comfort, and compassion. A house of refuge for all.

I am sad to say that many still have yet to find it. Jasmine wasn't looking for people to help, she wanted to help herself, but this was what God wanted Jasmine to go through for herself as well as for Him. We need to stop thinking that everyone is lazy and doesn't want to work. Try walking a mile in another man's shoes, and you will discover that there are things that arise in life that we somehow can't control. This is one of the reasons why we go through trials, so that we can learn to help others who get into our situations while remaining our sensitivity too.

I know many of us are struggling to make it. Some more than others, but God wants to get more to us.

Jasmine knew that everyone around her may not have either, but that's the beauty of it. Everyone helping everyone (**2 Corinthians 8:13-14**). Everyone caring for each other no matter how much they have or don't have. Jasmine also knew that many did and would not part with a dime or a meal. Jasmine felt and understood what God was trying to get her to see as she became a living witness to His truth. She felt the heartlessness of His people towards one another. She saw the priests and the Levites in many people. They just passed by her as if she were not there.

It amazes me how we rush to get in line when some big name comes to town and sow seeds of faith hoping that God will give us a big return. Is there anything wrong with that? No and Yes! No, If the lines of needs in our churches, our communities, and our schools are not neglected. Yes, if there are lines of needs in our churches, our communities, our schools that go neglected. What am I saying- "Charity starts at home!"

Everyone knows someone and more than likely we know more than one person that is going through an ordeal in his /her life. We offer them prayer, our sympathy, but we hardly ever meet his/her need.

Why?

Why do we refuse to depart with things? If someone is hungry, feed them. If you have money, then share what you have. Giving is not limited to money only. Time is also a commodity that we can give. Our talents and gifts are too. Maybe we can offer to pick someone up for church, take them shopping for food, or even baby-sit for them sometimes. All of this will help the person who is going through. There are many examples in the Bible that teach us to give.

"Give and it shall be given back to you with good measure, pressed down shaken together shall men give into your bosom."
Luke 6:38

We say it in church every opportunity we get, yet when we must complete the act we fail to react.

Think about what life would be like if each of us saw a need that we could help fulfill. The Levite and the priest were no strangers to the Word. Am I saying that there are people who go to church every Sunday, there every service, and still act like this? Do I really need to answer this question? Well, Yes, there are and unfortunately too many. We have our bumper-stickers on our cars. We even speak "Christianise ." Still our hearts are like stone.

All of them should have opened their refrigerator doors and given to Jasmine. She should have so much that she doesn't know what to do. Some could have given up their Sunday weekly night at the restaurant to feed her family. Everyone should have come together to support her, but only a small few did and most of them were not of the faith, who offered assistance without the need to ask.

So where do they go if they cannot come to the house of God?

THE WORLD!

Many go back into the world, and the world should

never have the edge on giving more than church. The church needs to step up and do the work of the Lord. They need to become "true" worshippers. Instead the church has gotten caught up with programs and agendas that we have overlooked the needs of the people. There are plenty of souls that need to be saved; therefore, no church should be empty. There is plenty of money in the church, so why are so many still without? The world should see the church as the strongest and most vital institution on this earth. Instead the church has become a local organization with no affiliation to God in stepping up and leading the way.

Where is the church?

Arguing over who should speak in tongues or not. Who has the bigger church with more members and how much money can we collect in an offering?

Oops!

Did I say that!

You darn right I did because it is time that the truth

be told. Too many churches taking in loads of money from their own people, and their congregations are in poverty, in need, and despair. It should not be.

I believe that a pastor should live well, but not at the expensive of its members. If your house is in order then that's one thing, but if it is not then get in order, and I am not talking about your physical house- The one you call home; the one where your wife and kids abide at. I am talking about the House of God.

Does everyone in that House of God have what they need?

If your natural house needed bread to eat would you take the money and buy a new suit? No! Then why are so many in the house without while the pastor is getting a new car each year. There is no way that you should get anything unless you know everyone in your house is taken care of.

Before a dime leaves to take care of anyone else's needs, the church needs to make sure that the people who support it are taken care of too! Too many times I have seen pastors live well while people who do not have, sacrifice money and time so the pastor has. The pastor should feel the same way about the sheep that God has given to him to feed.

Don't pray for big churches when you cannot meet the needs of the current congregation. Stop living beyond your means. Taking on more debt and expecting the people to pay for it the expense of them having o lights, no food, no cars, and some no place to live and you know you they are not going to let you live with them. Pray that God give you wisdom to seek the kingdom of God and His righteousness and He will add to us (**Matthew 6:32**).

Before any man can be called a Deacon or Bishop his house is examined. These positions have qualifications that man can use to identify the character of someone who wishes to become such.
If this qualification is befitting for a Deacon and a Bishop much more is required of the Pastor, the Apostle, the Teacher, the Evangelist, and the

Prophet. I am pretty sure that these ministry positions are positions that are appointed by God, that God himself has set some requirements for them. Even though the roles of the five ministry gifts are clear (**Ephesians 4:1-13**); the qualifications God uses are not clearly stated in the Bible other than by His divine appointment.

I heard a story about a church where the Pastor and his congregation came together to pay off each other bills so that they could be free from some of their debts. Now I know that they did not pay off their houses, but I am not sure about their cars.

However, all of their other bills created from credit cards were paid off. With everyone being semi-debt free, more money was available for the kingdom and the work of the ministry. The house taking care of the house so that it is in the position to help others. Again, this is scriptural too, because **2 Corinthians 8:13-14** tells us this.

I like that. It fills me with joy. I hope one day to meet this pastor because what he did was awesome. This gives me hope, and lets me know that there are those in the faith that are doing the will of the Father. Hopefully, this will inspire others to do the same that we all can be on one accord. Woe to those who will not *give* to help one another.

With all of this money going into the churches every week, I am sure that we should somehow be able to help others. With one heart and mind, we should be able to come together for the common good of the Gospel. Yet we don't. The church is divided instead. There is only one God, one faith, and one baptism (**Ephesians 4:5**). God is not the divider of the churches with different beliefs, preaching a different doctrine. One reason is because of lack of knowledge. God tell us that His people (Hosea 4:6) will suffer because of it.

On the other hand, some of us are setup by the adversary to divide and conquer. To steal, kill, and destroy the mission of the church and the true Christians (**John 10:10**). There is only one Holy Bible from which mankind has derives all sorts of misconceptions and notions about the truth in God's Word and many of us have bought heresies into it. It is called tradition. Jesus never followed the traditions of the Pharisees or the Scribes. Many could say He was a rebel with a cause. So WAKE-UP!

"It is time for the church to get themselves in order."
The Author

Chapter 5

Embracing The Gift of Sacrifice

The greatest sacrifice known to man is the sacrifice God gave us when He laid down the life of His Son, Jesus, for the remission of our sins (**John 3:16**). The Bible tells us that there is no greater love than when a man lays down his life for a friend (**John 15:13**). Yet, so many of us struggle with the mere thought of sacrificing material things, compassion, love and money each and every day.

This chapter will help us to understand what a true sacrifice is so that we can become better givers and doers of God's Word.

What is a Sacrifice?

I researched the definition of the word sacrifice in the dictionary and I found that it offered multiple meanings of the term. The two most relevant were:

(*1*) to sell at loss and (*2*) the act of giving up one thing for the sake of something else. Both meanings can be used to support the meaning of the sacrifice Jesus made on the cross over 2000 years ago. However, there are still many misconceptions about what a true sacrifice is and why some believe that you can only have plenty to give, but that is not true.

A sacrifice can be made when you don't have plenty to when what you give is given at a loss to you. Jesus' death on the cross is a perfect illustration of a true sacrifice. Jesus gave His life in hope to gain our life- Lives that were eternally damned, yet this act of love for us, cost Him His. A gift of love that we should never take lightly, but we do. Jesus' sacrifice is by far the most perfect example the Bible could offer us, but the Bible doesn't stop there. It is filled with scriptures, upon scriptures about others who made great sacrifices for numerous reasons.

Let us take a brief look at the story about the woman who gave two mites.

"Jesus had looked up and saw the Rich man casting their gifts into the treasury. And he saw also a certain poor widow casting copper coins (two mites). And he said, of a truth I say unto you, that this poor widow hath cast in more than they all, For all these have of their abundance cast in unto the offerings of God; but she of her poverty hath cast in all the living that she had."

Luke 21:1-4

We have just read that this woman had given all that she had. She could not go to the bank and get more. She wasn't going to get a paycheck on Friday. What she had, was all there was, and **she gave it all**. A true sacrifice by every means!

On the other hand, the rich men that were casting their gifts into the treasury are examples of some of us who give, not a loss to us, but think that what we gave is a great sacrifice. God calls it only an offering.

How does this relate to us today, right now?

Well, let us continue to look at Jasmine's life trial to

see if the principles concerning the woman with two-mites is relevant to us today.

We have learned in the previous chapters that Jasmine was facing a serious emotional and life changing trial: a trial involved her learning to depend on God as her true and only real source. In the development of this lesson, God has posed a question to Jasmine asking her "Who is Thy Neighbor?" This question forced Jasmine to focus and examine her life more closely. What Jasmine discovered was that the neighbors who God was talking about consisted of everyone who surrounded her at this given point in her life. She also came to realize that her life was paralleling that of the Good Samaritan.

During this trial, Jasmine's source of income was, at first, dependent upon a wayward husband who did not perform in his role as the provider most of the time. How did Jasmine survive thus far? By divine intervention from God. God used friends and enemies alike to bless Jasmine and her children during their times of need. With all of this in mind, we will now look what Jasmine did with the little bit of income that God did place in her hands.

When Jasmine had little to nothing, the little that God provided for her, she still gave more than 10%, the tithes and offering, back to Him. Her obedience to giving did not stop there, but went even further. One day when Jasmine's husband returned home to serve God, he and the neighbor across the street went out witnessing. While they were witnessing to a young woman, they invited her to church with them that Sunday.

She accepted.

That Sunday she came with her daughter to church, and she surrendered her life to the Lord. After the service, Jasmine's husband invited them over for dinner at their house.

Now, they did not have enough food for themselves so, this presented a dilemma for Jasmine. She did not want to turn them away. She saw that this young lady still wanted to be in their company. However, she could not believe that her husband invited someone over knowing their situation.

So, Jasmine let the invitation that he made stand. When they returned from church, back to their home, Jasmine offered the young woman a seat, sent her child upstairs to play with her children, and went into the kitchen to begin preparing the dinner. Jasmine began seasoning meat which consisted of seven chicken drumsticks. Then, she began to marinate the meat to be stewed.

As she began marinating the chicken, the family from across the street stopped by. As the family entered Jasmine's home, the husband, went upstairs to talk with Jasmine's husband while the wife spoke with Jasmine in the kitchen.

She watched as Jasmine was preparing dinner and asked if she had enough for everyone.

Jasmine said, "No, not really"

Then explained that she was fasting anyhow, something she did not intend to do.

The neighbor replied,

"If she had enough, she would give them, but they were running low themselves."

Jasmine understood and continued to prepare the meal.

Afterwards, they left the kitchen to let the meat marinate a little while longer.

As they were about to enter the living room where the young woman had been sitting watching TV, her neighbor turned and went upstairs to see what the men were up to and to check on the children.

About 15 minutes later, Jasmine returned to the kitchen to stew the chicken and as she was placing the chicken into the pot, she noticed that the amount of chicken had increased. She counted the pieces of chicken again and again.

Suddenly, Jasmine let out the loudest yell- "Thanks-you Jesus!"

At that moment, the anointing of God fell upon her

and she fell to the floor. When Jasmine began to open her eyes, they were all standing around her asking what she had yelled for.

Jasmine, still a little shaky, began to tell them what God had done. With her spirit making her feel like she was floating on clouds and her hands and body were still shaking. Jasmine heard the Lord say to her, "I fed 5,000 men with five loaves of bread and two fish, what more will I do for you (**Luke 9:12-17**)?"

She heard His voice while she was trying to explain to the others what had happened. She could see their faces as she was trying to tell them what God had done. Her neighbors were joining in to help her give God praise for what He had done while her husband had doubts and began to question her.

As Jasmine started to stand, everyone was still rejoicing.

Then her husband said,

"You must have miscounted the pieces."

Jasmine replied,

"No, I did not. I can count to seven."

Remember, in those days, Jasmine did not have much money to shop for food. She could only purchase so much. When she shopped, she would always get this box of chicken from the same store which always consisted of twenty-one pieces of chicken. She would then separate them into groups of seven, counting food to see how many days each would last.

On this day they were down to their last seven pieces. Her husband really did not know, most of the time, about the amount of food they had. He was hardly ever around, but her neighbors from across the street knew because they were very supportive of her, during this trial.

As Jasmine was trying to explain to her husband that she knew how much was left, her neighbor's wife interrupted the conversation to confirm that

Jasmine's count of the chicken was correct (**John 5:30-31**). The neighbor explained that she was in the kitchen at the time of preparations, and she confirmed that there were only seven pieces of chicken in the bowl that held the marinated chicken.

The men finally left the kitchen and went towards the front door. The women still gathered in the kitchen talking about the miraculous thing God had done. There were 12 pieces of chicken, enough for everyone who had to eat, and God did it.

The woman from across street and the young woman left the kitchen to return to the living room where the men were. This left Jasmine in the kitchen alone still continuing to prepare dinner. As tears were streaming down Jasmine's face, the voice of the Lord spoke to her again and said- "Because of your willingness to sacrifice and go hungry for someone else, today you will eat with them too."

Jasmine fell again. Now, what is this to say, I would like to think that it would be obvious, but just in case it is not, here it is. It is our faithfulness to give in lack that will make us rulers over much (Matthew 25:21).

Not only did she see the miraculous hand of God at work in her life, but she learned about giving. That day changed Jasmine's life towards giving and towards God. She learned to give not only when she had, but even when she did not. Every time there was anyone in need, there was an opportunity to give. It does not matter what their circumstances are and you really do not need to know all the circumstances anyhow. You just need to give. Jesus even told us to feed our enemies (**Romans 12:20**).

Jasmine was never the same after that day. She had experienced something that no man could take credit for. No one could say that they had brought extra food. No one could say that they gave money to buy more. No one could say that they were used to bless her. God had done a miracle for her. Her life was changed forevermore.

Now, let us relate to the Good Samaritan. This

Samaritan did not know what this certain man's situation. He did not know how this happened to him or why.. What he saw was that he was wounded. What he saw was that he was dying. What he saw was that the man needed care. He saw that he had no money and apparently no ID because he is called a certain man, Ha! Ha!

Why did this man not have a name? I believe that God wanted a person that could reflect anyone, Man woman or child. He never saw a need, and he fulfilled it. He did not stop there either. He took him to an inn and told the innkeeper to bill him for whatever this man will continue to need. No questions asked.

Most of us do not like to get involved with too many people that we do not know because it really isn't our problem, but theirs right? We don't mind hearing that gossip about them, but ask us to do something to help. Well, that depends on what you mean by help. Money help, most don't like to do.

However, we don't have any problems giving

something old, worn or something we did not want anyhow, but try something you just bought. That's a different story. Let it interfere with the plans, that we have to buy something we really want and do not need, anyway. Again another story. We have become so cold and hard-hearted towards people that giving unconditionally, just because it's right, is difficult.

Now granted we do have some true giving Christians and churches that do great things overseas and a few of them at home. Many of them are supporters of different ministries too, but what about our home front. The people right in front of us every day. How many of them get overlooked? Just because we live in a country that gives the opportunity to be wealthy doesn't mean it is given to everyone. If it's a God problem, then it is ours too.

Sometimes we will see the man on the corner with a cup, dirty, and hungry. Maybe we will give him a dollar or maybe we won't. What decides this? Sometimes our mood. If we are having a good day or a bad day. Sometimes how much we have on us that day. We may only have a few dollars, and we will need gas during the course of the week so we need to hold on to it. Sometimes we say, "God didnot place it on my heart"- This is my all time favorite. Sad to say, they are right. He may not have placed it on their hearts, but I guarantee it that He placed it in His Word for us to live by:

"And before him shall be gathered all nations: and he shall separate them one from another, as a shepherd divideth his sheep from the goats. And he shall set the sheep on his right hand, but the goats on the left. Then shall the King say unto them on his right hand, Come, ye blessed of my father, inherit the kingdom prepared for you from the foundation of the world.

For I was hungered, and ye gave me meat: I was thirsty, and ye gave me drink. I was a stranger and ye took me in Naked, and ye clothed me: I was sick, and ye visited me: I was in prison, and ye came unto me.

The righteous answer him saying, Lord, when saw we thee hungered and fed thee? Or thirsty, and gave thee drink?

When saw we thee a stranger, and took thee in? Or naked, and clothed thee? Or when saw we thee sick or in prison, and came unto thee?

And the King shall answer and say unto them, Verily, I say unto you, Insomuch as ye have done it unto one of the least of these my brethren, ye have done it unto me.

Then shall he say also unto them on the left hand, depart from me ye cursed, into everlasting fire, prepare for the devil and his angels:

For I was hungered, and ye gave no meat: I was thirsty, and ye gave me no drink: I was a stranger, and ye took me not in: naked, and ye clothed me not: sick and in prison. And ye visited me not. Then shall they also answer him saying, Lord when saw we thee a hungered, or a thirst, or a stranger, or naked, or sick, or in prison and did not minister unto thee?

They shall he answer them, saying, Verily I say unto you, Insomuch as ye did it not to one of the least of these, ye did in not to me."
Matthew 25:32-46

Now, it is plain for us to see what the Word says about giving and helping others. Believe me the Word says much, much more; too much to list.

The Word tells us to give, and it shall be given..., and to give to the poor, yet some use the excuse that they are waiting on God to tell us to give, when to give, and who to give it too. That's utter Nonsense! Let us be real if anything else. Some are not waiting on God to tell them anything. They are just being stingy, money misers who just won't let go. They use this as an excuse to not give because God should lead us in all things.

I am not saying that God will not lead us in our giving, but there are some things that we should just know to do. When someone is hungry we do not have to wait for God to tell us to feed them **(James 2:15).**

However, if someone came asking for $10,000 because God told them to come, I would seek the Lord first before I did it? Rightly dividing the Word of truth.

Jesus told the Gentiles to seek ye first the kingdom of God and all its righteousness and all these things we seek will be added unto us **(Matthew 6:33)** because God knows that we would become lovers of material things. He also knew that it would be that same love that would keep us from receiving the best from Him. He knew that, so He wrote about it in His Word to give us wisdom about ourselves and that we would not become lovers of these things. That is why Jesus took from the unprofitable servant and gave to the one that was profitable.

"Take therefore the talent from him, and give it unto him which hath ten talents...."
Matthew 25:28

That is why some of us do not see the full blessings

of God or any blessings at all. We sow sparingly, and we reap sparingly (**2 Corinthians 9:6**). We sow nothing, and we reap nothing. We hold on to the seed that God has given us to sow. Read the parable of the sower (**Mark 4:3-25**). Our jobs are not our source, but an opportunity for us to have seed to sow. Everything we own is the Lord's, and if God tells us to give it, we must be willing to give it no matter what the cost or how much we worked for it. All is the Lord's! This is troubling to many of us because we know this is theory but not in operation. We have dummied down this commandment to just a cliché' like we have done so many of God's truth. We have rendered it powerless.

Question?

Could there be such a thing as "careful" giving? You know when they say that you must be careful who you give too. I believe that this "careful" giving is a double edge sword. Why? Well, because it is true that we must be careful in all things we do. We must be led by the Spirit of God. On one hand, I believe that we should seek God before we make any move. Onon the other side. I believe that people use it with the motive to limit giving or not to give at all. So I guess what I am saying is that it is the motive for giving that determines how God views your obedience in this area.

Careful defined means any things such as *cautious*, *attentive to potential harm* or *danger*, as well as *anxiety* and *protective* to name a few. So depending on how you use it will determine your motive or actions towards God.

Jesus, our example, was he a careful giver or did he give to everyone? He made the sacrifices for us when we were yet sinners, and He still died for us. Were we deserving of such a great sacrifice? No, because there was nothing good that we could have done to earn it. His sacrifice was selfless and he gave His life as a ransom for all willing to receive it. The greatest example of love ever for us to follow. Then God gave of us the unique gifts of the Spirit. They are ours if we obey Him or not (**Romans 11:29**) because our gifts are irrevocable.

The Word also tells us that if we ask, it shall be given to us (**Luke 11:9**). No qualifications to meet. No appointments necessary. Even those with the wrong motives, God gave mercy and told them to sin no more. The adulterous woman who they were going to stone. She was dead wrong and caught in her sin yet, Jesus protected her. Jesus fed 5,000 men not including the women and children, who we could bet were not all there for the right reason, yet He fed them.

Judas is another example of this- He stayed in Jesus' presence, and Jesus knew that he would betray Him. I do believe that there is such a thing as careful giving in the fact that we must be led by the Spirit of God, but I do believe that it is often used as an excuse not to give or to give too much either. Many justify their giving by saying that Jesus tells us to be good stewards over what He has given us and this is true.

In the Bible, Jesus tells the disciples a story about an unjust steward (**Luke 16:1-13**). One day this steward was asked to give an account of his stewardship because it was reported to the Master that he was wasting his goods. To make a long story short, the steward tried to cheat the Master by having those that owed the master adjust their bills. In other words a cover up. This way it would appear as if he did not misappropriate the money. Although, the steward was commended for his shrewd act, the Master evidently did not approve of it.

The bottom line is this. If you are going to be dishonest with what God has given you, then know for sure that it will all blows up in your face. The unjust steward's willingness to cheat the Master made the debtors happy, but not the master. It was the steward's Master who supplied him with the goods from the beginning, but he still tried to cheat him. Some of us are no different. We try to short change God every opportunity we get. The steward was robbing the Master who is God. Will a man rob God (**Malachi 3:8**)?

Every day, we use the seed money that God has given to us improperly. By this, God means that we use what He has given foolishly: buying things we really don't need; wasting it in an ungodly way, like buying liquor, sex, cigarettes, and so forth. Yet, we struggle to give or tithe. We need sacrifice some of the material things we want so that we can be in a position to give. Then, and only then, will God see to it that we have the things He wants for us. If we practice this order we will receive from Christ the abundance that He promises. It is while we are handling God's business that God is handling ours. Seek God First!

We should use money to yield more money, unlike the profitable servant, and be careful of how it is spent. In regard to being a good steward, giving is a sign of being a good steward. Giving yields more fruit (**Luke 6:38**). Remember, Jesus walked the earth pouring from His spirit to anyone and everyone who had a need. Should we do the same?

Of course this does not pertain to the entire body of Christ. There are a few of us who have come into this revelation of God's law for giving. It's the rest of us who need to get on the ball with it, if we plan to receive the best from God.

We must not concentrate on what we have or do not have. Do we really trust God when we sing Jehovah-Jireh, Lord my provider or is it just a song to be sung?

Relax and Release it! Where ever your treasure lies so does your heart also (**Matthew 6:21**).

Chapter 6

BLESSED OR CURSED, YOU DECIDE!

As you can see, God is very serious about giving. Giving is an act of kindness, love and compassion. The Bible tells us that God loves a cheerful giver (**1 Cor. 9:7**). He doesn't want our sulky money. Money giving grudgingly. He wants you to give cheerfully because you love Him and want to obey Him. In all that we do for God, we should do so wholeheartedly and without haste.

Giving is also a source to wealth and prosperity in Christ Jesus (**2 Chronicles 1:12**). The true Christians must come to the understanding that in order to obtain wealth, God will empower us. Once empowered, we must be willing to share what we have (**1 Timothy 6:17-19**).

In this chapter, we will examine how God feels about those whom He entrusts with wealth and material things and what happens when we unselfishly give or when we don't. Giving can bring about either blessings or curses in your life. A blessing comes about when we give and because of our willingness to give unselfishly; God adds more to us. On the other hand, a curse comes about when we selfishly hold back, and God subtracts from us and gives to others who are willing to share.

Earlier, I mentioned the parable about five talents (**Matthew 25:14-30**). This is a prime example of God's sowing and reaping principles, plus it illustrates how giving can affect our lives. In the parable of talents, a man traveling to a far country calls his servants so that he could deliver some of his goods to them. He trusts each servant with a different amount of talents. Some received five, therefore, another two, and to another one, but each according to his own ability.

When he returned after a long time, he settled

accounts with them. The one with five talents had gained five more. The one with two talents, gained two more, but the one with one talent hid it in the ground which brought forth no gain. Therefore what he had was taken away from him and given to those who had. He was considered an unprofitable servant.

God knows how much we can handle. He is not going to give us a dime, if we cannot handle a nickel. God understands just what we can handle and will not add to us until we are mature enough to handle it.

Our seasons are divided into sowing and reaping. A time when we will plant and a time when we will gather up what we have planted. This man had sown some seeds (talents) by giving each servant a trusted amount. Although he gave a talent, he did not give them the same amount. Each servant received according to his own ability.

Now that intrigued me so, I looked up the meaning of the term "ability." According to the dictionary, the word ability has two meanings: (**1**) the power or means to do something or (**2**) a natural skill or talent.

In retrospect of the scripture, the term ability, in context, indicates that the man gave each servant based upon the power or means that they have to do something. In other words, each servant received according to his/her capability, competence or qualification. How the man determined this is not revealed to us in the Bible, but if think about how we conclude our decisions, then we can safely rationalize a number of possibilities from one level to another level because God's thoughts are higher than ours (**Isaiah 55:9**).

After a long period of time, the man returned to gather the harvest from his investment. For the most part, he reaped from those wise and profitable servants, but from the one who did not provide a profit from what was given to him, he did not and his was taken away. God does us the same way. If we don't prove ourselves to be profitable with what He has entrusted us, the same result hold true for us.

Although, this parable has been interpreted in many ways, God revealed it to me like this. God, represented as that man in the parable, trusts each of us with money, houses, cars, and even the souls of people. Some of us receive more than others, but we each receive according to our own ability. God does this so that we can prove ourselves to be faithful servants with what He has already given us. We ask for more, He looks to see what we have done with what we already have. If we did not use it wisely, then what we have will be taken away from us and added to those who did. It is as simple as that. God told us to bestow what we have to help the poor.

"His Lord said to him, 'Well done good and faithful servant; you were faithful over a few things, I will make you ruler over many things."
Matthew 25:21

Jesus, one day, entered and passed through Jericho.

He came across a man named Zacchaeus who was a chief tax collector, and he was rich. Zacchaeus wanted to see Jesus so much that he climbed a sycamore tree just to see Him. When Jesus saw him, He instructed Zacchaeus to come down. Zacchaeus stood and said, "Look, Lord, I will give half of my goods to the poor, and if I have taken anything from anyone by false accusation, I restore fourfold (**Luke 19:1-10**)."

Jesus replied- "Today salvation has come to this house because he also is a son of Abraham". Abraham was called the Father of Faith. He was also a very wealthy man. God made a promise to Abraham and his seed. He vowed to bless Abraham's seed with the same blessings that He bestowed upon Abraham.

Now what made Zacchaeus a seed of Abraham? It is obvious that Zacchaeus was not adherent to God's laws because when Jesus told him that he would stay at his house, many heard this and complained saying; "Jesus has gone to be a guest with a man who is a sinner." But, notice that after Jesus told him that he would stay at his house (His invitation of salvation), Zacchaeus was willing to pay back four times the amount to those he cheated and willing to give half of his possessions to the poor. It was his willingness to give and to repay (with interest mind you) that led to salvation for his home that day. He was willing to give up his old life with those old ways. Hint! Hint! Imagine what would happen to us, true Christians, if we gave up things unselfishly and without cause to help others. We would receive the abundant life.

Earlier, I mentioned that God wants us to feed His sheep (John 21:15-17). This can be done both naturally and spiritually. Most of us believe that this scripture was meant for a pastor because his job is to feed the Word of God to his flock. Although this is true, this task is not limited to the pastor and neither is it just meant for us to feed them with the Word. He also meant for us to feed them if they are hungry naturally. God wants us to look out for one another both spiritually and physically. Some of us do and some of us don't- Either way there is an outcome to face. Those of us that obey will receive rewards. Those of us who don't will have our rewards taken away, but not after many opportunities to correct our mistakes. With numerous chances, many still refuse to conceive God's will. Many of us are just hardhearted and selfish. We just won't share. As true Christians, we must be willing to share what we have in abundance or not. Don't be caught on the curse side of the blessings just because you are afraid to let go of your possessions. **Luke 12:15** tells us that a man's life consist not in the abundance of the things which he possess.

"Take heed and beware of covetousness for one's life
Does not consist in the abundance of the things he possesses."
Luke 12:15

Those of us who have accepted this principle will receive or already have received from God more than our share and possibly yours too, especially, if you are not a willing and cheerful giver. Let's look at what God says about those who do not give.

"For we brought nothing into this world and it is certain we can carry nothing out. And having food and clothing with these we shall be content; and into many foolish and harmful lusts which drown men in destruction and perdition.
But those who desire to be rich fall into temptation and snare, For the love of money is the root of all kinds of evil, for which some have strayed from the faith of their greediness, and pierced themselves through with many sorrows."
1 Timothy 6:7-10

Now some of us may be looking at this passage and wondering if God wants us to be rich. Well, He does! God delights in the prosperity of His servants.

Let them shout for joy and be glad, who favor my righteousness cause; And let them say continually, "Let the Lord be magnified who has pleasure in the prosperity of His servant."
Psalm 35:27

God states in 2 Corinthians 8:15 that He that gathers money slowly, to him will there be no lack because what he wants will last. But, those who rush to gain wealth, normally through deceitful means, will fall into temptation and snares. They will make foolish decisions out of greed, creating sorrows and eventually losing what they have (**Proverbs 13:11**) and have nothing left over.

We can see this in our society. Look at the world's method for obtaining wealth, it is crumpling. Everything we have valued and put our trust in is falling apart. Stock markets are down. Businesses are closing. Embezzlement is on the rise. People are losing their minds over money and material things. People are committing crime after crime to obtain the American dream: wealth, expensive cars and fancy homes. Little do they know, the wealth of the sinner is laid up for the just (**Proverbs 13:22**), but only those who are righteous in the sight of God will reap the harvest. Giving is one of those righteous acts. The Bible tells us this about giving.

"Give and it will be given unto you: good measure, pressed

down shaken together, and running over will be put into your bosom. For with the same measure that you use, it will be measured back to you."
Luke 6:38

Notice the scripture says, "With the same measure we use, it will be measured back to us." So think about what you want measured back to you. More money, then give money. Houses and land, then give houses and land. The Word says that whatever we sow, we shall reap.

What is wrong with getting rich quick?

Lots of things. For one, God wants to make sure that the money we have does not control us, but that we have control over it. The Scriptures tell us that the love of money is a root to all kinds of evil (**1 Timothy 6:10**). You cannot serve God and mammon at the same time (**Matthew 6:24**).

Money is man's greatest weakness and dearest possession. Do you want to know how many times I have heard people say that money was evil? Too many to count. Preachers for years have gotten this statement wrong and have taught many of us to think that money was evil.

Unfortunately, we have churches today that still believe this very thing. They have deceived their people into thinking that Jesus was poor and that this is the way we should all be. They have gotten people to sell their possessions for the sake of wrong preaching and teaching. People have lived deprived and poor lives with no hope to obtain the true promises of God because of these teachings. Meanwhile, those same preachers, pastors or reverends drive around with Cadillacs, and live in nice homes at the expense of their congregation members. What's sad to say, is that some of us still believe this lie today.

Money is not evil. It is a commodity. How can a piece of paper be considered evil? How about the magazines and catalogues we buy, are they evil too? It is not the commodity that is evil, it's the love of it. Let me say it again. It is not the commodity that is evil, it is the love of it. It is mankind and its ways that make money evil. It is the way money is used and valued in our society that also makes it evil. Not only have we become lovers of it, we have make it our god. Wars are started over it, and crimes are committed to obtain it. People kill themselves everyday working for it in order to obtain material things. We are no longer in control of this green paper because it now has control over us. People are selling their souls just for the sake of it. It is ridiculous and insane to be that desperate for a green piece of paper.

How can something that God created take control over us? Easy, by giving it more value that it is worth. By worshiping the money instead of the Creator of money. Nothing and I mean nothing can be more valuable than our relationship with God and the salvation of our soul. Many have traded their souls for money and they pay the price.

There is nothing wrong with riches and wealth. God wants us to prosperous and wealthy.

"And you shall remember the Lord your God, for it is he who gives you the power to get wealth that He may establish His covenant which He swore to you fathers as it is this day."

Deuteronomy 8:18

The Word commands those that are rich not to be haughty, nor to trust in uncertain riches, but in the living God, who gives us richly all things to enjoy. He says: let them do good, that they be rich in good works, ready to *give*, willing to *share* (**1 Timothy 6:17-19**). That we should not store up treasures for ourselves here on earth. God's Word tells us in **Luke 12:20-21** that he that layeth up treasure for himself is not rich towards God, for who can say when their soul will be required of them and then where would all of it be. Life is more than meat, clothing, and money. Life is all these things that the nations of the world seek after. God knows that we have need of these things. The Bible tells us in **Luke 12:31** that God would rather we seek the kingdom of God and then all those things shall be added unto us.

Money is a necessary commodity for the trade of goods and services, but when we get to the place where we are dying over it naturally and spiritually, we must begin to look closer at ourselves individually and as a society. Once we begin to obey the Word of God like we are supposed to, then many of us will begin to see greater blessings from God.

"But, seek the Kingdom of God and His righteousness and all these things will be added to you."
Luke 12:31

Recently, I had been talking with a friend about God. She began to tell me how she now serves God from her home and refuses to go to church anymore. I asked her why and she told me a story about the church that she once attended. Because of the delicate nature of this story, names have been omitted.

Apparently, she was hurt by the church that she attended on a regular basis. She had been going through a serious financial trial on her life, when one day she went to her pastor for some assistance with her bills. She and her children were close to being evicted from their home. She said that she had been faithful tither. She had attended church with her children on a regular basis and participated in the choir. When she met with the pastor concerning her situation, the pastor offered her prayer and told her to seek new employment elsewhere. Even though, this was sound advice, it did not meet the need she had. She needed money right away otherwise they would be living on the street.

What got under my skin when I heard about this situation was that she had been a faithful member of the church. She may not have had a strong foundation, as some of us, but she was on her way. Her experiences was like when a parent abuses the child who trust in them, because he/she does not know any better. It was after this experience that she felt she no longer wanted to be a part of this church or any other. Where were the true Christians? Who is thy neighbor?

Unfortunately, we deter many good people this way. All of us do not enter this Kingdom walk at the same time; therefore, some of us are not strong in the Word and in the discernment of spirits. Based upon whether the doctrines are sound, many are taken advantage of and abused. Many get tossed to and fro with the wind and end up back in the world because they did not see the difference in us. Many get discouraged by the actions or should I say lack of action from some of our so-called churches of God. Where are the true Christians? Who is thy neighbor?

Pastors all across the world teach the principles of sowing and reaping as well as giving. They teach their congregations to be cheerful givers and that giving is the key to prosperity and wealth, but is the church eliminated from the responsibility to give just the same? God forbid! We are supposed to be the examples for the world to see. They should see our giving and want to be just as we, but this is not always the case.

We have outreach ministries for all sorts of overseas countries, but fail to have one for those at home. I am not suggesting that we don't have these outreach ministries for overseas countries, but how can we feed the hungry abroad and see the very ones in front of us starving. The church should be a place for restoration, deliverance and healing, not just emotionally and spiritually either. Financially too! Instead many are wounding wounded people who are looking for the church to be different from the world. Where are the true Christians? Who is thy neighbor?

It is churches like this that gives God's name a negative report. This causes the world to see the church as a money-hungry institution, taking the people for gain and profit while giving nothing or very little back. This may not be true for all of our churches, but unfortunately it takes a few bad apples to spoil the whole bunch. That's the enemy's plan.

What we understand to be an attack of the enemy, the world however does not see nor understand these spiritual matters. They only believe what they see and hear. The media loves to grab hold of people to make the church of God look like crooks. The media deters others from coming and seeking us for help. The world will look to find fault with Christians and the church. So, we must be mindful about everything we do, say, and everywhere we go. For example, just going to pay a bill at a liquor store. Harmless right, wrong! Although you are not doing anything wrong, your appearance in an ungodly environment will cause people to assume and normally they will assume wrong. God tells us to abstain from all appearance of evil (**1Thessalonians 5:22**). Meaning, we should not give Satan a place to attack us. It saddens my heart and grieves my spirit when I hear about churches who have turns their backs on the same people who they need to survive. When the church does not pour back into the people that are making the investment, we have a serious problem. Where are the true Christians? Who is thy neighbor?

The church should be the source of giving. If the world is to learn anything, it should learn from the church, but instead we are adopting the world's attitudes and its ways. God called us to come out and be separate (**2 Corinthians 6:17**) - Not to follow the ways of the heathen. For He has also chosen the foolish things of this world to confound the very wise (**1 Corinthians 1:27**). Have we become as fools?

Let me leave those of you who are afraid to give with this in mind. It is a scripture that I feel sums it up.

"There is no need to fear when times of trouble come, when enemies are surrounding me.
They trust in their wealth and boast of great riches.
Yet, they cannot redeem themselves from death by paying a ransom to God.
Redemption does not come so easily, for no one can ever pay enough to live forever and never see the grave."
Psalm 49:5-9

The Examination

Who Is Thy Neighbor? was written to examine the heart of the Christian soul. Overall, it's purpose is to perpetuate our readers to examine their hearts to see if there are any black or dark hidden areas in their giving that would stump their spiritual growth and hinder them from receiving the blessings that God has in store for them, but the examination is not limited to just your giving. God wants to examine all areas of your life just the same.

Many of us enter into this Christian walk with lots of worldly perceptions. Our perceptions have been formed from societal, environmental as well as our traditional upbringing, adversely affecting and influencing the way we live our lives. Some of these perceptions can be easily erased while we struggle to overcome others. It is my hope and faith in God that this book will help you overcome those things that so easily beset you so that you can walk a victorious life.

Psalm 26:2 tells us that God puts us on trial to cross-examine and test our motives and affections so that we can be declare our innocents when He judges the world. God desires, in these days, is to free us from all those ties that bind us. Whatever stands between you and the place God has called you to be, He wants to move it. You will find others, such as myself, who will write or preach messages that will convict, chasten, rebuke, and reveal hidden areas of your lives that have gone unnoticed or just not dealt with. God said that there is nothing hidden that would not be revealed (**Luke 12:2**). This includes our sins and our shortcomings.

Some of us are better givers than others, but we all have something that is hard for us to give. Please understand that giving is not limited to just money, but includes the giving of time, love, compassion, skills, talents, and so forth. Some of us are great givers of time. We will help around the church doing whatever is necessary, but find it difficult to give money. Others may be great givers of money, but won't give their time- Either way we have something to hurdle and work through. We must ask God to open up our hearts and examine those dark areas- Wanting God to loose those ties that bind our hearts. Once we know what hinders us, God can perform His surgery. As we cry out "Lord create in me a clean heart," God will begin to mold and shape us into His true vessels of honor. God's surgery can sometimes be painful to us. His surgery may place us in situations that requires us to exercise exactly what it is we need deliverance from. For example, if we are impatient, God will place us in situations that will exercise our patience. But, sometimes our ego, pride, and stubbornness gets in God's way, creating an unwillingness to let go.

We all mean well, but when we refuse to become the givers that God desires us to be, we can become bound by greed, worldliness, selfishness, or haughtiness, making us as stingy misers. Regardless of the spirit(s) that hinder us, God desires to set us free. This battle we face involves the souls of people. In order for the world to see God, they must first see Him in us and through us. Too often the world is made to look more attractive than God's people especially when it comes to prosperity. The drug dealers are stealing our youth and destroying our homes, but they make money. Big business men with power suites are stressing out the lives of people for profit and gain, yet we push our children to be like them. The requirements to obtain wealth in the world is not the same as to obtain it in the Kingdom. So, what is one way we can be sure to represent God in finances? **GIVE!** It is through our giving that God's love is shown to the world. The world gives mostly for selfish reasons like a tax write-off. God's people should give because we love him.

This is why God is demanding us to change our ways. We must make up our minds one way or the other to serve Him. Either we are for Him or against Him (**Matthew 12:20**); there is no in between. We cannot serve two masters (**Matthew 6:24**); we either love one or despise the other. The two masters that God refers to is money and Him. He is separating the wheat from the tare. Our heart and our willingness to submit will be the deciding factor. By now, we should know that God's people are identifiable by their love towards God and one another. Love is the character above which all other fruits of spirit are obtainable. If we love with the love of God, we can be kind, merciful and full of compassion towards one another.

I have made one prayer request to God concerning the publication of this book and that is for God to deliver and set free all those who are willing to read this book and be obedient to the Truth that He has chosen for me to reveal. I wanted this book to bring freedom to those desiring a change in their lives. God promised me that He would. He promised that if you would be obedient and complete this examination that He would deliver all of you who have a sincere heart and the desire to be free.

Right now, before you continue to red on, I would like for you to stop and ask God to show you where you have fallen short in your giving. Ask Him to reveal those deceiving and deceptive spirits that hinder you from receiving the fullness of His blessings. On the lines below write down those things that god has shown or spoken to you so that you can have a record of these things God is faithful in doing for you. Now with a sincere heart, pray this prayer and include those things that God has given or shown you.

Father,

Because you love me, I thank you for the opportunity to become what you desire me to be. Forgive me for I have sinned. I have not done those things that you require your servant to do. I have been selfish and self-centered. Lord, you said in your Word that whatsoever I bind on this earth, shall be loosed in heaven. Today, I pray that you bind those spirits of _____, _____, and _____ that keep me from receiving and fulfilling the call that You have placed on my life and the blessings you have stored up for me. Loose the spirit of compassion, love, and discernment.

I know now that it is your desire that I live my life according to you will and your ways. I know that you have called me to be blessed so that I can be a blessing to others. By your spirit and the authority obtained through the blood of Christ, I cast out of my being any unclean spirits that are not like you.

Create in me a clean heart and renew in me a right spirit. A spirit of giving and a spirit of love. I give unto you all the praise, all the glory, and all the honor. In Jesus' name I pray. Amen.

Receive now the blessings in your life. Prepare to receive the blessings that God has stored away for you. Ask what you will from the table that God has prepared for you in the presence of your enemies. Believe that you will and have received all that you desire from Him, and God will bring it to pass.

Now, if you would do one more thing. Drop us a line to let us know that you have completed the examination. We will include your response card in our daily devotion prayer and will stand in agreement with you for all that God has for you. I hope that you will be blessed the same way God has blessed me! Remember to send the examination card right away!

Chapter 7

WRAPPING IT UP

Well, we have finally arrived at the end of our journey. Much has been said, and I know many of you are filled with food for thought, but before I go let us just make sure that we are clear about God's law for giving and how the parable of the Good Samaritan is a manifestation of the fruit we should parody.

God expects us to give and it is just that simple. **Matthew 5:42** tells us to *"give to him who asks you, and from him who borrow from you do not turn away."* With this in mind, note that the borrowers should not be the Christians. God's Word tells us that we should be the lenders, and not the borrowers (**Proverbs 22:7**) because a borrower becomes a servant to the lender. In other words, the world should borrow from us. Instead, we borrow from them which makes us slaves/servants to their financial system. This is why many of us are in so much debt and this is why we need to be in financial control of this world. As rulers of the financial world the world's unrighteous world be in debt to us and we could apply the principles that God gave us concerning giving, loaning, and interest.

On the other hand, when we lend to our brothers and sisters in Christ and expect repayment, we enslave them to us as borrowers. This should not be. We should give to them and never put them in the position of a borrower. I believe that we should never be in debt to each other. Again the house taking care of the house. Giving, tithing, and being good stewards over what God has given each of us now will put us in this position. Instead we are subject to the rich in this country who are not godly in character, therefore we are slaves/servants to them. The good news is that the tide is about to turn. The greatest transfer of wealth, in history, is about to take place. God is preparing His people to receive the wealth of this world. Your stewardship and giving plays an important part to receiving it.

God has given us no excuse for not giving. We can

no longer say to God that we do not know because with what we have just read, we are now held accountable. Giving is an important aspect to receiving from God. There is no longer a way around this expectation unless we choose to remain in disobedience. The Bible is filled with many blessings that derive from our act of giving. **Luke 6:38** says, *"give and it will be given back to us good measure pressed down shaken together and running over will men give unto your bosom"* With no hesitation, reading this scripture should encourage us to be faithful givers and enormous ones at that. Just knowing that the measure in which we have given comes back to us multiplied makes me want to run and leap over mountains. I do not know about you, but that sounds like good news to me. News that makes you want to shout for joy.

Although many of us give, many of us are still not cognizant, physically or mentally, of the fruit from our giving. This is because of the attitude that some of us may have towards giving. God wants us to be cheerful givers. He doesn't want sulky money. I mentioned that in one of the earlier chapters. Giving willingly, cheerfully, and with a pure heart is the key to unlocking the doors. We should never give for the wrong reasons. Many of us give looking for something to come back to them. This is wrong. **Acts 20:35** tells us that it is better to give that to receive.

Paul was talking to the elders at Ephesus when he said to them: As an Apostle of Christ, I had the awesome responsibility of setting up churches all over the world. I was responsible for teaching the principles and the laws governing the salvation, the blessings and the gifts that derive from a relationship with Jesus Christ. When Paul dealt with the elders from Ephesus, he knew that they would never see him again, and he wanted to make it clear to them that they should follow the ways of our Lord Jesus Christ. The same way we ought to become imitators of Christ, His Ambassadors.

Again looking at the reasons why so many of us are prolific with our giving is because many of us announce what we do for others all over town so that Men will notice our good works and God tells us in **Matthew 6:1**, *"Take heed that you do not do your charitable deeds before men, to be seen by them. Otherwise you have no reward from your Father in Heaven."* Let me say this part again, no reward at all. I emphasized this again because we need to get this into our hard heads. Stop looking for Man to notice us and to bless us. It is all about God and what we do for Him is to bring glory to His name, not ours. There is no big "I" in you. So, if you have been doing this, it might explain why you have not received your rewards.

Yet, the Bible does not stop there. **Matthew 6:2-4** continue to say, *"Therefore when you do a charitable deed, do not sound a trumpet before you as the hypocrites do in the synagogues (churches) and in the streets, that may have glory from men. Assuredly, I say to you, they have their reward. But when you do a charitable deed, do not let your left hand know what your right hand is doing, that your charitable deed may be a secret; and your Father who sees in secret will Himself reward you openly."*

This means keep your giving to yourself. You need not announce it all over the place. Your life will reflect your giving by the reward that you receive from God and men will know that you are blessed. God will want them to know it because when He uses your life as an earthly example of who He is and who He can be to others, you better believe that God will let the whole world know it. Isn't that good to know that we can become a part of His fruit here on earth?

Giving is an act of love, kindness and compassion. These attributes that represent the God we serve. It is because of these same characteristics that God gave us the greatest sacrifice known to man; the one Christ made when He gave His life on the wooden stake for us. Christ did not have to make that sacrifice at all. In the Garden of Gethsemane, Jesus prayed that the cup not pass away from Him. Regardless of how He may have felt in His flesh, He submitted Himself to the Father's will anyhow. This is how we should respond to everything the Word of God tells us to do. We should want to do the will of the Father in all things, even when it comes to our money, and our possessions. We need to stop holding on to articles that we cannot take at death nor use to gain eternal life. These material things are perishable.

The question still remains, "Are you the Good Samaritan that the parable tells us about?" If not, do you want to be? If you do not, then I will let God deal with you, but for those who do, it will require a great deal of sacrificing from you to become like this Samaritan. This Samaritan was a sacrificial giver. He went beyond the normal donations that we often give. HE went beyond the dollar or two that we normal give to someone we see on the streets. He actually secured another man's future. How many of us would pick up someone we do not know, take them to a hotel, pay all their bills, and then tell the clerk at the desk, "Here is my credit card. Bill it for whatever he will need the rest of today, tonight, and tomorrow." Who knows how long he had to care for him and it really didn't matter? The point is he did.

I can see some of you now squinting your faces just at the thought. Some of you are actually thinking that he was foolish. Others are saying, well he must have been rich. Why is he foolish? Why is it that only a rich man can perform such a sacrifice? Truly he hasn't.

Remember the story about the young rich man in the book of **Matthews**, chapter **19** verses **16-23**. This young rich man wanted to have eternal life so he said to Jesus, Lord, I have kept all of God's commandments. Jesus replies that if he wanted to be perfect, that he should go and sell what he has and give it to the poor, and then he will have treasure in heaven and could come and follow Him. The young rich man went away sorrowful because his wealth was great. Jesus responded that it would be harder for a rich man to enter into the kingdom of heaven than it would be for a camel to go through the eye of a needle. Why? Not many rich men I know make such sacrifices. They may give, but their giving does not impact on the amount of wealth that they have obtained. What they give is just a drop in the bucket to them, but a whole lot to us. In order for them to sacrifice, they must be willing to give at a loss to themselves. Which means to sell all. The same way Jesus gave His life as a ransom for ours (**Mark 10:45**).

I am not saying that we should all give away our riches as fast as we get them. That was not the point to the parable. This was a test of where this man's heart lied. Would he be willing to sacrifice all that he had for eternal life?

This was no different that when God asked Abraham to sacrifice Isaac, the son God had promised for many years that he and his wife Sarah would have. God was testing Abraham, and He was testing this young rich man. He will test us also. It is not the riches or wealth that God is interested in, it is the motive and intent of our hearts. The willingness to be obedient to His will. God wants to know where our heart lies. That's why being faithful over all things is important (**Matthew 25:21**). It is our faithfulness in what we have now that will increase what we have later. God wants to know that He can trust us. If He requires us to give all, would we. This is the place Abraham had to come to and this is the same place God wants us to come to. This is why Abraham is called the Father of Faith. It took a whole lot of trust and love for God for him to even consider, needless to say putting his son on an altar and be willing to sacrifice him. Imagine having to do that. We quiver at the thought of sacrificing our money and material things.

This young rich man, like most rich people, could afford to give and not make a dent in his pockets. This young rich man like most rich people, gave to the poor and what he gave did not hurt him in anyway. Jesus knew that in order for the young rich man to make a sacrifice, he would have to sell it all and give it away to the poor. That is why he walked away sorrowfully. Just the thought of having nothing and losing all of his wealth made him sad. To do it, he would become like the people that he was giving too, poor. He probably could not stand the thought. Jesus knew what his reaction would be, but he told him to do it anyhow. Like most things done in the Bible, it was for our good. To see the rewards and the consequences of our obedience and our disobedience and to help us identify with ourselves and see where our changes are necessary. There are many matters that others had to bear, that we will never come close to bearing. The same way Jasmine's experiences are for our learning too.

Notice the different between the young rich man and Abraham. One was willing and obedient, while the other was unwilling and disobedient. Now, look at the outcome of each lives, Abraham and his seed inherited the promises of God, and the young rich man walked away with his possessions in tack and without eternal life. What does it profit a man to gain the whole world and lose his soul (**Mark 8:36**)? NOTHING! Isn't this what God's Word tells us. How about you? Would you be able to give all you had to the poor? Would you lay down your life for a friend? This is why God wants to make sure that the wealth He gives us does not have us under its control, but that we will have control over it. Money gained through dishonest means is money that will not last. Money gained through our worldly devices will not last either because the wealth of the wicked is laid up for the just. People with overnight success and no character don't stay wealthy for long. That is why God adds to us nice and slowly, when we have proven ourselves worthy of the increase.

God told us about the treasure of money and the love of it. If money controls us, then we will have a hard time letting it go. We will become misers, stingy, and haughty over it. If we gain it too quickly, it may be so overwhelming for us that we cannot handle it. Our motives must be right. If they aren't, we will use it incorrectly, and waste it on superficial things. Look at the lives of some of our popular stars and singers. Many of them came from the church, but became enticed by the quick wealth of this world. Lured by the deceitfulness of prosperity, too impatient to wait on God to open up the doorway to their success, so they have compromised their beliefs to perform songs for music companies that are not gospel related and to perform in shows that do not uplift the name of Jesus. All this for the dollars of this world. Because of their disobedience, many of their lives have been ruined by alcohol and drugs as well as lives filled with sexual exploits. Some have even gone bankrupt because they wasted their money on superficial material things that they cannot take with them. Even the pressures to keep up with the world overtakes them, and they end up messed up and some even die in their sins.

The Word tells us in **Mark 8:36**, for what does it profit a main to gain the whole world and lose his own soul? That is what has happen too many of us and will continue to happen too many of us when we make money our god. The young rich man could not depart with his wealth in that he gave up the chance to have eternal life. How about you? What have you given in exchange for your soul (**Mark 8:37**)?   Money and material things aren't the only things that we can give in exchange for our soul. Many things stand in the way of God being first in your life. It could be your children, success, a boyfriend, a habit of some kind, and more. Nothing and I mean nothing should separate you from the love of God. You should say this to each obstacle in your life, "Lord not even this!"

When it comes to sacrificing, personally, I do not think sacrificing has anything to do with being rich, middle class, or poor. Sacrificing can happen at any financial level. Different financial levels only determine how much we can give but don't be fooled, one can give more with little that one with much. Giving is giving wither way. It is our attitude towards money and the material things we obtain that makes the difference. Our problem begins with the fact that we value them too much. We live in a society where material things are used to classify people. People are defines by the material things they own or how much money they make. God did not decide if we were worthy of eternal life by the things we own. He did not classify us as His children by how much money we have. He said that you know his people by their love, which is His love, for God is love. With confessions of a pure heart we accept Christ into our lives and we are forgiven. There is no financial requirement necessary.

However, God knows that an evil generation seeks a sign, but no sign will be given except the sign of the Son of Man as Jonah was for the Nin'e-vites (**Luke 11:29**). We are the ambassadors to Christ (**Ephesians 6:20**), the Son of Man. He now abides in us so that this evil generation can see us as they see Christ, Son of Man. We should strive to imitate Christ in all things.

Although we are not perfect, this is why we must strive to free our minds and submit our ways to

God's will for our lives. When we do this, God's people will see the signs and wonders that His words said should follow those of us that believe (**Marks 16:17**). For some of us this is already happening or about to. They have uncovered God's principles, and they obey them (It's not that they were hidden either). We just hadn't been looking closely enough or we just didn't want to let go of something yet.

Normally that's what it all comes down to. What are you willing to change and sacrifice to be in obedience to God's will and to receive the blessings that He has already prepared for you. Some of us are not waiting on God to bless us meanwhile, God is waiting on US: waiting on us to line up with His will and to His ways. He has already prepared a table for us filled with all of the promises and blessings. Many of us approach this table, but cannot take anything from it. In order to know why we must submit ourselves to God and what it is that we must do in order for us to obtain what it is we want, He will tell us.

I want you to think about something and I mean really think about it? Why are there so many different churches with different beliefs? Is it because God likes variety? Is it because God is confused about what He wants? Not at all. It is because of man's willingness to accept or reject God's laws and principles. I believe that we have so many different churched with different beliefs because we have decided only to accept what is comfortable and what we are willing to give up. Other than the obvious reasons, you know that Satan has deceived the church. Sin has prevailed. I truly believe that Satan gets far too much credit for decisions that man has made governing themselves.

We must also remember that God is our Source, not our jobs- Other people or even societal organizations that supply financial support. We are soon coming to the place where we will have no other choice, but to depend on God to live, to move, and to have our being (**Acts 17:28**). This is why we practice it now so that when those times come, we will be strong in God and able to stand. The world's system and all that it has created is about to crumble. If your hope, and your faith is built on anything else, but Jesus blood and righteousness, then you will crumble with it.

I heard some of you saying what about tithing? Doesn't my tithe constitute as giving? Yes, you are right, it is your giving and your rightful service. Tithing is very important. God requires us to tithe a tenth of our possessions. Whatever it is that we have. To bring all the tithes into the storehouse that there may be food in God's house, the church (**Malachi 3:10**). In the Old Testament they tithed everything that they possessed. What are you saying? Is tithing just limited to money? No! We can tithe our time, our talents, and our skills as well. All is the Lords.

I believe that we can tithe a tenth of our time to shelters, and any other organizations that may need our assistance. We can even a tenth of our talents and skills to help others as well. For instance, if I was a builder and the church needed something to be built, I could use my skills to help them with no payment. Think about someone who does not earn an income to tithe. What will they give unto the Lord? In other words, we are using all that God has given us to help and assist each other. Even the world has gotten a hold of it. They just put it under another name. The world calls it *volunteering*. Giving up your time to help someone else. They even put value behind volunteering. So do not be afraid to tithe with all that you have. For God has not given to us a spirit of fear, but of love, power, and a sound mind through Christ Jesus (**2 Timothy 1:7**). Some of you may be thinking that this might mean that we can substitute. Sorry, you cannot do that either You cannot substitute your financial responsibility to give and tithe with other gifts and talents. Sorry! Nice try though! Tithing opens the windows of heaven. It pours out blessings that we may not be able to contain (**Malachi 3:10**). If we do not tithe we are robbing God and we become cursed- Something that we do not want to become. There are many good things that come with tithing. Things that I will not go into at this time, but if you want to know more continue to read **Malachi 3:11- 12.**

Tithing is major and you must tithe, but notice that God does not want us to stop there. He wants us to continue to give to anyone and everyone that ask us- to the poor and to all who are in need. Although tithing is majorly important it is not all that God requires from us. We cannot substitute tithing with giving to the poor. They are not the same. Each with has its own benefits.

Giving to the poor has many benefits. **Psalm 41:1-3** tells us that we are blessed when we consider the poor. As a giver to them, God will deliver us from trouble, keep us alive, and will not deliver us over to our enemies. Even on our bed of afflictions, He will strengthen us. Aren't these promises just great, for considering the poor? The promises are too good to pass over. Maybe some of us would live longer and be in better health, if we gave to the poor more often and more sacrificially.

Since the poor will always be among us (**Mark 14:7**), we will have plenty of opportunities to give and to help them. This will give us plenty of opportunities to receive those blessings that come with it too. For that fact, the poor are so important to God that He said to invite them to dinner before inviting anyone else (Luke 14:12-14). He said not to ask your friends, your brothers, your relatives, nor any rich neighbors because they will also invite you back, and you will be repaid. If they repay you for your act of kindness, then it is not charitable or sacrificial to you. What you do for others should yield no reward for you and not just due from them, otherwise, it is an even trade.

When you do give a feast, invite the poor, the maimed, the lame, the blind, and you will be blessed because they cannot pay you back. Let's go back to the fact that it is better to giver than to receive. Now it does not mean that you cannot have dinner parties with your friends, family, or rich neighbors. It means open our house once in a while to others who are in need and who you do not know. If you do not want to open your house, then go out and invite some who are misfortunate.

Remember, Jasmine was poor. No one offered to take her out to dinner nor invited her over. Instead they went out with their friends and relatives. They all faithfully prayed and encouraged her, but that did not satisfy the hunger she was facing. The Good Samaritan helped the man who helpless and needed care. By now it should be clear that God's desire is for us to give. Giving has it blessings if we do and it curses if we don't. Now that you have examined all the evidence, I hope that you will join those of us who have caught on to this principle of sowing and reaping. I hope that you will become a Good Samaritan and be recognized by God as a good neighbor. Remember you will reap if you faint not.

Man of you may not agree with what is said and many of you will; either way, that is fine because the Word tells us not to be easily offended. When God called me to walk in the position as an inspirational and motivational writer, one of the tasks He chose was for me to write were books that would set free His people because He loves them. He prepared me to face opposition from the church, even the world. It is also my love for you that I submit my will to that of God's so that He might be glorified through me.

His hope is to finally get us to walk in Truth. Walking the complete Truth of God's will for our lives. It is time. When Jesus came among the Pharisees and Scribes, the religious leaders of that time, He convicted them. They thought that they had understanding when they did not have any. I know that you are not really in disagreement with me but with God and the wisdom and knowledge that God has given to me to interpret His Word. I am but an Ambassador of Christ, charged with the task of speaking the Truth of the Gospel, Armed with the armor of god. For this I am guilty. For telling the truth I am not.

I give no offence in anything, that my ministry may not be blamed. In all things I commend myself, as a minister of God: in much patience, n tribulations, in needs, in distress, in stripes, in imprisonments, in tumults, in labors, in sleeplessness, in fasting; by purity, by knowledge, by longsuffering, by kindness, by the Holy Spirit, by sincere love; be y the Word of truth, by the power of God, by the armor of righteous on the right hand and on the left; by honor and dishonor, by evil report and good report; as deceivers, and yet true; as unknown, and yet well known, as dying behold I live; as having chastened and yet not killed; as sorrowful, yet rejoicing; as poor, yet making many rich; as having nothing and yet possessing all things. Oh, true

Christians! I have spoken openly to you, my heart is wide open. If you are restricted it is not by me, but you are restricted by your own affection (**2 Corinthians 6:3-12**).

I pray for your and hope that one day you will see all there is that God wants you to know. Above all things, my desire is that you prospers. It is the truth we know that will truly set us free. Until we meet on that glorious day, be blessed!

Jasmine's Story

Jasmine learned many things from the trials that she faced, and we should have learned something too. Jasmine, although a fictitious character, faced real situations. Situations that you and I or someone else has faced, is facing, or will face at some point or another. Jasmine is a representation of many of us. Her feeling and emotions are feelings that some of us have felt many times over.

The story and the events you have read are true. They actually took place. The names were changed or eliminated to protect the innocent and the guilty. This story was not told for your amusement or entertainment, but so that lives could be changed: yours as well as mine. I have shared with you the life of a friend who bore stripes for you and me so that we did not have to bear them. We should learn from her victories as well as her defeats. We should learn from her fears as well as her courageous acts. She has done none of this to receive your recognition or your praise, but so that Christ might be glorified through her.

Many of you may still be wondering how things turned out for Jasmine. Well, Jasmine's trial continued well pass the point of this story. Many more miraculous things were done in her life by God. Jasmine, eventually did get a job, and she and her family moved from the residential area in which she lived. She stood on the Word of God and all that she desired at the time came to pass. She holds dear her memories and testimonies that developed form these trials.

Although she did not enjoy the pain and hurt that she endured during the trial, what she does hold dear is how God revealed Himself to her in a miraculous way as he wishes to do with most of us. Many of us do not get to see the miracles in our lives. What we considered miracles is something that could be explained naturally. For example, needing food and someone comes by out of the blue with what you need. They are miracles in their own right, but not the true miracles of old. You know the ones that cannot be explained and leave Mankind wondering how did it happen. God still does these miracles today.

Jasmine walked away from her trials blessed, both spiritually as well as physically. You can say that God blessed her more in the latter than He did in the beginning. Jasmine continues to tell many testimonies to those who would listen. It did not matter who they were. All she needed was an open door to speak to you. She testified of God's goodness to her so that others would be encouraged to press on to reach the victories in their own lives.

Jasmine stands anchored in His love towards others. She is committed to doing His will His way for life. As a warrior for the Lord and willing to place her life on the front line for the Gospel sake, not compromising the Word for the sake of the things in this world, she deems her soul too important to gamble with.

Jasmine is a sheep in God's flock, and God continues to Shepherd over her life, even to this day. She stands strong in God and in the power of His might. Knowing that she has done all to stand, she continues to stand some more until her race is finished and until she hears God say, "Well done my good and faithful servant."

God left Jasmine with one scripture to live her life by and to remember why she went through hard places. It is this scripture that the Holy Spirit uses to remind her of why God has placed her in such difficult positions that only God can get her out. This is something that she wants to share with you.

"To whom much is given is much required."
Luke 12:48

Jasmine bears these things for you so that the knowledge and wisdom that she acquired from them, she has now given to you so that you won't have to bear these things too. Remember it is taking in the accurate knowledge of the true God and His Son that leads to everlasting life. (**John 17:3**) Peace Be Unto You!

You therefore must endure hardship as a good soldier of Jesus Christ. None engaged in warfare entangles himself with the affairs of this life, that he may please him who enlisted him as a soldier (**2 Timothy 2:4-5**).

A
Prophetic
Psalm

No temptation has overtaken you except such as is common to man; but God is faithful, who will not allow you to be tempted beyond what you are able, but with the temptation will also make the way of escape that you may be able to bear it.

1 Corinthians 10:13

Life's Constant Roller Coaster Ride

Life is a constant roller coaster ride
Filled with curves and turns, lows and highs
For some don't mind the rides filled with thrills
while others prefer to remain calm an still

Either way, life is going to offer us both the same
A ride filled some joy, sorrow, laughter, and some
pain
We must learn to embrace ourselves
For a ride with unknown
"Cause it is there whether we embrace it
or just moan and groan

There are paths in life we all have to face
Regardless of our profession, our status, our creed
or our race
God never promised us a life with no storms
but He did promise to guide us though it with no
danger or harm

We are expected to mature and grow during
those bumpy and uncomfortable times
'Cause there is wisdom to gain from every one
of our tears and from every one of our whines

God promised to put no more
on us than we can bear
but while we are there, know that
He loves us and that He cares

"Excerpt From A Father's Love"

Be diligent to present yourself approved to God, a worker who does not need to be ashamed rightly dividing the Word of Truth.

2 Timothy 2:15

Reference Guide

Scripture References

Here is the list of scriptures used in the book.

Love

Seasons

John 13:34-35

Ecclesiat. 3:1

1 John 4:30

Galatians 6:5,7

Luke 6:27-28

James 1:2-4

Salvation

Joel 12:25

John 3:16

Fear

John 15:13

Proverbs 1:7

Mark 10:45

Psalms 2:4

Servanthood

Psalm 49:5-9

Galatians 5:13

2 Timothy 1:7

1 Corinth. 4:1

God Ways

Luke 16:13

Hebrew 13:8

Psalm 100:2

Genesis 6:3

John 12:26

Hebrew 10:19-20

Ephesians 6:20

Revelation 3:8

1 Corinth. 10:24

Hebrew 6:19

Matthew 6:24

John 15:5

Luke 11:29

Ephesians 4:6

Deuter. 13:4

John 5:30-31
Deuter. 11:13-17
1 Corinth. 10:26
Luke 10:37
Isaiah 55:9
John 14:15

Rewards

Heart

Luke 6:30-35
Proverb 4:23
Genesis 12:2

Cares

Matthew 6:32
1 Peter 5:17
Matthew 25:21

Sacrifice

Proverb 2:4-7
Ephesians 3:11-12

Change

2 Corinth. 5:17-21

Changes

Giving

Psalm 55:19
Matthew 5:4
Jeremiah 18:3-6

Luke 6:38
Mark 8:3-7
2 Corinth. 8:13-14
Matthew 8:23
Matthew 25:32-46
1 Corinth 3:1-
3Matthew 6:33
James 4:8
1 Corinth. 9:17

Parables & Stories

2 Chronicles 1:12
Luke 10:25-37
1 Timothy 6:17-19
Luke 21:1-4
1 Timothy 6:7-10
Luke 19:1-10
Luke 12:31
Luke 16:1-13
Matthew 5:42
Luke 9:12-17
Acts 20:55
Matthew 25:14-30
Matthew 6:1-4

Living Holy

Mark 4:3-25

Romans 12-1

Mark 14:7

Acts 17:28

Luke 14:12-14

Knowledge/Wisdom

Malachi 3:10-12

Proverbs 1:5

Psalm 41:1-3

Luke 12:12

Consequences

2 Timothy 2:15

Psalm 37:9

Proverbs 1:7

Revelation 3:19

Matthew 7:16-20

Ephesians 6:1-3

Hosea 4:6

Matthew 25:25

Temptation

Overcomer

1 Corinth. 10:13

Jeremiah 32:7

1 Corinth. 1:27

Philippians 4:13

Battles/Flesh

Luke 12:15

Ephesians 6:10-18

Gifts from God

Isaiah 54:17

John 17:3

Romans 8:35

Psalm 145:18-20

John 10:10

Psalm 65:2

Gifts, con't

Luke 12:20-21

Romans 11:29

Psalm 35:27

Faith, Hope & Trust

Proverb 13:22

Proverbs 3:5-6

Proverb 13:11

Isaiah 40:31

Ministry Gifts

1 Corinthians 5:11

Psalm 32:8

2 Thessalonians 3:14-15

2 Timothy 4:5

Matthew 25:21

Deut. 18:18-22

Study

Jer. 3:15; 10:21

2 Timothy 2:15

1 Corinth. 9:1

Warfare

Ephesians 4:11-13

2 Timothy 2:4-5

Roles of God

Ephesians 4:14

Jeremiah 31:32

2 Timothy 3:16-17

Psalm 68:5

Examine

Rejection

Psalm 26:2

Luke 10:10

The Great

Commission

Doing the will

Matthew 28:19-20

Romans 7:19-20

The Golden Rule

Knowledge

Matthew 7:12

2 Timothy 3:15-17

Babes

1 Peter 2:2

Old Testament

Exodus 19:22

Job 1:1-12

Exodus 15:22-27

Exodus 16:1-35

Wealth

Deutronomy 8:18

Mark 38-36

All About Me

"I wrote this under the inspiration and anointing from the spirit of God to validate and celebrate who God is and can be in each of our lives. I pray that we realize that truth is not something to be taken lightly. It is this truth that will set us free."

About The Author

A native of the great city of New York, Monique R. Ransom is a mother of four gifted & anointed children (Sierra, Tyrone, late Trenton, Renee), and a dedicated teacher in the Baltimore City School System. She graciously draws from the Lord's Spirit, inspirational books filled with astonishing words and motivational messages that will encourage, uplift chasten, and provide hope for the soul.

Educated in New York Public School System, she graduated with a Business Degree from Adelphi University. It wasn't until her first child was born that she became inspired to seek a career in education. She adds to her list of accomplishments a Master's Degree in Education, but her greatest accomplishment was on March 12, 1989 when she accepted Jesus Christ as her personal Lord and Savior.

Through grace and faith in the promises of God, she and her husband are now the renown business owners of Praise Wear International's Gift Shop, Glory Enterprises Unlimited Ministries.

Together, the family works to provide just a little bit of heaven in each of your lives.

Given this vision from God over ten years, Monique ministries from her heart and soul to those who have gone astray; to those who are broken hearted; those who are imprisoned in their minds while inspiring others to fight the good fight of faith.

Each word written or spoken is an expression of God's infinite wisdom which she obtained from her own trials and tribulations. The prayers and anecdotes that she uses to combat her own challenges and the hardships that she faces daily in her life, she now shares with us.

So, journey with her as she opens the gates of hell to set the captives free.

Our Mission

In our journey through life there will be many challenges to face, many decisions to make, and moments when we will embrace the unknown. Circumstances will bring about changes to our plans. Dreams will sometimes shatter. Hope will be destroyed and our faith will sometimes fail us. It is in those moments with the unknown that we will wonder if we are standing alone. God, our Father, wants us to know that He loves us dearly. He knows when we need just a speck of hope; or a glimmer of light to shine its way with solutions to what ails us.

Through our ministry, we hope to provide healing, deliverance, and restoration to the mind, body and soul of each person we come in contact with. Our ministry's mission is based around Isaiah 61:1-4.

The spirit of the Lord God is upon me Because the Lord has anointed Me To Preach good tidings to the poor; He has sent Me to heal the brokenhearted, To

proclaim liberty to the captives, And the opening of the prison to those who are bound; to proclaim the acceptable year of the Lord, And the day of vengeance of our God; To comfort all who mourn in Zion, To give beauty for ashes, The oil of joy for mourning, The garment of praise for the spirit of heaviness; That they may be called trees of righteousness, The planting of the Lord that He may be glorified.
Isaiah 61:1-4

It is this scripture that inspired us to seek and plow through the bowels of the earth to find those who have gone unnoticed by the world and make them Disciples of Christ.

Letting them know that they do not have to settle for where they are right now in their lives. That no matter what they have done or how many mistakes they have made, with God it is never too late. Only with men are things impossible, but with God on your side all things are possible if you only believe.

We hope to get the opportunity to encourage you too!

MORE ENCOURAGING
AND LIFE CHANGING
WORDS BY THE
AUTHOR

MONIQUE R. RANSOM

A FATHER'S
LOVE

DECLARING GOD'S GLORY!

A Father's Love
A Poetic Book of Psalms

CAN A CHRISTIAN BE POSSESSED BY AN EVIL SPIRIT?

Monique R. Ransom

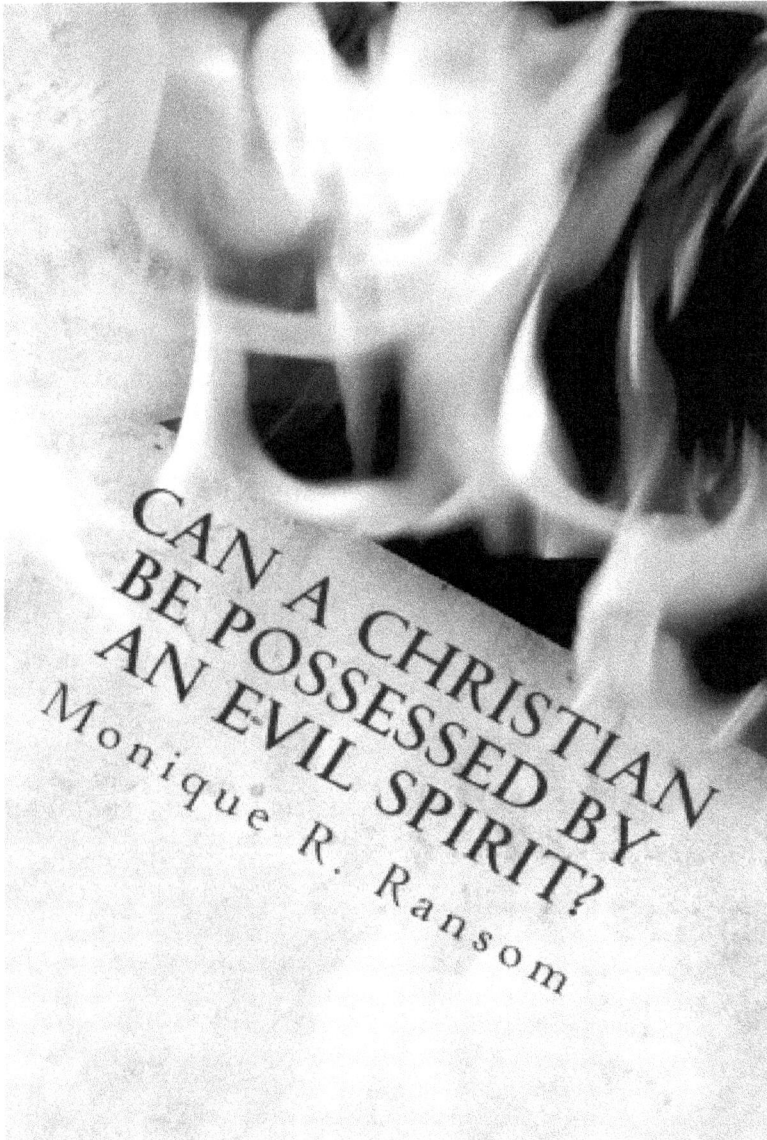

Don't let the title fool you. It deals with our twist of God's words.

Through His Grace and Mercy Thou Can Be Saved!

The Bible says, "That if Thou shalt confess with thy mouth the Lord Jesus and shall believe in thine heart that God raised Him from the dead, Thou shalt be saved. For with the heart man believeth unto righteousness and with the mouth confession is made unto salvation." (Romans 10:9-10)
If you would receive Jesus Christ as Lord and Savior of your life, with sincerity, pray this prayer from your heart:

Lord Jesus,

I believe that You died for me and that you rose again on the third day. I am a sinner and I need Your love and forgiveness. I invite you into my life, forgive my sins, give my life its meaning and make me whole again. Give me eternal life. I confess you now as my Lord and Savior. Amen

If you made this confession, we would like to hear from you.

Our Pathway for Communication is Now Open!

Reaching out to others is important to me. I would like to hear from you. If you would like me to speak at one of your events, to contact:

Write to:
FirstTouch Ministries for Women
P.O. Box 70126
Baltimore, Maryland 21237

On the World Wide Web:
Http://www.firsttouchministriesforwomen.com

Email:
shespeaks3@aol.com

Facebook:
www.facebook.com/she-speaks-wisdom

For more books and cd messages visit our web site.

www.ingramcontent.com/pod-product-compliance
Lightning Source LLC
Chambersburg PA
CBHW051825090426
42736CB00011B/1660